Tom
Madsen

Relentless

From Both Sides of the Veil

For—and with—Kevin.

I promised.

Everything recounted here happened exactly as described.
Selected names were changed for privacy.

Tom Madsen
Walnut Creek, California
May, 2020

Table of Contents

PART TWO

PROLOGUE

Role reversal

If a pearl had awareness, what would it sense and feel? Growing from a single grain of sand, in the dark, its needs are met, the rules and boundaries understood. But when its world is cracked open, and it is bathed in light, does it even have a frame of reference for the new experience? Does an entity which matured in the dark have a way of sensing the new light all around it? Freed from all the familiar touchpoints, how would it push and expand its awareness into this unimagined space?

Our world cracked open with Kevin's death. We blacked out, awoke on another planet, concussed, with no map back. We heard foreign, meaningless, incomprehensible sounds: *rules, right, wrong, should, need, fair.* Off-world and out-of-body, we saw our dull remains plodding through a faded pantomime of life, as if in a film projected on tissue paper.

I felt cut off and walled-in, under a thick, dark rubber membrane. At first I had no fight, lobotomized as I was in apathy and fatigue. The image of the rubber membrane settled onto me; I felt as if it even oozed into my pores. I could ward it off briefly with tasks or diversions, but if I sat or I lay down, if my mind went idle for a moment, it loomed nearby, stifling and smothering.

At some point, the survival drive came crashing through the door of my suffocating apathy. I *had to* resist this thing. I had to push through this membrane, to pierce it, if I were to have a chance. In my mind, I pushed against it. Harder and harder I tried to break through. I bored my fist, my shoulder, my head into it. Sometimes I thought I felt—or imagined I felt—it yield some. But I could never push through, and I needed to be on the other side, to breathe.

I can't say exactly when my primal need to push through this barrier transformed to a feeling of a pull. Maybe I needed to exhaust the urge before a new possibility could make me aware of its presence. A new image presented itself. I was still trying desperately to pierce the barrier. But now, off to the side, waiting patiently for me to tire and sense its presence, sat a benevolent energy, filing its fingernails. This wasn't a crisp image; I couldn't make out a clear person, exactly. I couldn't tell if this was male or female energy. All I got was this distinct impression of a figure, seated cross-legged, with the odd detail that it was filing its fingernails!

Is this *help*? A thought and a question tickled some part of my brain. It was clearly waiting for me to figure something out. What was I supposed to learn? Was it that my urge to push through this taunting barrier in the form of push-only was futile? That approach was too one-dimensional; it relied only on the physical. Was it too male, maybe? Oddly, this resonated, as if the question had been asked and answered—from where or whom, I couldn't say. But inexplicably, I trusted it.

During these months of questioning, pushing, trying—and yes, depression, sobbing, and lethargy—I felt Kevin. And he made his presence known to us on many occasions. So as I raised my head slowly from the muck and began to process these images and questions that entered my consciousness, I sensed Kevin encouraging me from the sidelines, as I had so often rooted for him at football, rugby, basketball, baseball, and soccer games. It never comes across audibly or visually, but as a feeling. And then I interpret the feeling with the only tools at my disposal: words. So for example, if I pursue a line of questioning that helps me think differently about how to push through to the other side of grief, I may get a feeling which, when put into words, says "That's it!"

Just posing these questions seemed to crack open something new: a window of gradual understanding, maybe. Hard to say. And the fact that it is hard to say will frustrate our usual selves, the selves who have been raised and anchored in the physical, the logical, the Cartesian view of the world and the universe. I am neither physicist nor metaphysicist, but I feel certain that what is becoming available to me is not measurable nor discoverable from the realm of our familiar touchpoints. It is not responsive to our usual frames of reference. To go there—I think—requires intuition, trust, empathy, and most of all a kind of openness we were never taught.

I imagine that I've lived most of my life with maybe one percent of the universe available to me. Lately, I feel that maybe I'm at seven percent! But so as not to mislead, nothing I have just shared magically solves or cures grief. But I've come to believe that grief is not meant to be solved or fixed. Grief is the yang to Love's yin. The quality of one drives the depth of the other. In the West, we seem to believe that bad feelings must be made to go away. Maybe we have it all wrong. Maybe the burnishing of the soul *requires* us to go through pain, death, grief, and poverty; as well as to experience love, beauty, wealth, admiration. Maybe that's why we keep coming back.

No, we will grieve for Kevin the rest of our physical lives, because our physical selves miss him so much. We won't see his college graduation, his marriage, his kids, his dreams manifesting. But that grieving is for *us* and what we miss. We know that Kevin is fine where he is. He watches over us, and he lets us know he is well and happy. So we grieve still, but the nature of the grief shifted. We can see a life after grief, or maybe more precisely, a life *with* grief but not *consumed* by grief. Our lives have not stopped. We can move forward and even find a happiness with a different quality.

And that heavy rubber membrane? That image doesn't trouble me anymore. And I do feel...lighter.

PART ONE

Hello There!

We first saw Kevin on a sonogram live screen image when Marilene was seventeen weeks pregnant. We were at the Kaiser hospital in Oakland, California, in March 1998. This would be our first child, so it was all new to us. Going in, we knew nothing. Was the baby healthy? Boy or girl? Growing on-track? You go in with an intoxicating blend of joy, anticipation, heightened wonder, with a little fear thrown in. What if it's not all okay?

After we completed the forms and spent a few minutes in the waiting room, they brought us to the ultrasound examination room. Marilene went behind a curtain and changed into the loose green gown. Soon the technician came in and greeted us warmly, sharing in our excitement. She smeared the cold gel all over Marilene's rounded abdomen and ran the ultrasound sensor over the gel. After a few seconds of maneuvering, an image began to form on the monitor next to the bed. The technician spoke.

"Okay, five fingers on each hand. Five toes on each foot. So far, so good. You want to know the sex?"

We said we did, yes, please.

"Well, you're going to have a little boy. Congratulations." I would have been happy either way, as long as the baby was healthy. But I'd be lying if I said I didn't prefer a boy. Marilene and I beamed at each other.

As the technician moved the sensor around on the gel, the image of Kevin alternately sharpened and fuzzed. Finally, she settled it to a spot that satisfied her. She signaled for us to look.

We saw movement. The technician described how we could see Kevin's heart beating in the middle of his chest. We could see the little walnut-sized sac pulsing, pumping. It was such a thrill, I thought I might pass out from joy.

"What's going on here?" I asked. We could see a rhythmic movement around where Kevin's cheeks and mouth were.

The technician maneuvered the sensor slightly to sharpen the image around Kevin's head. "He's sucking his thumb," she said. "Don't see that every day." Sure enough, we could make out his right arm up and his little thumb in his mouth, the cheeks hollowing a few times, pausing, then resuming. We could see his heart pumping at the same time we could see him sucking his thumb!

The rest of the examination proceeded—at least as far as the technician was concerned—routinely. After confirming that all seemed to be going normally, we wrapped up the appointment, got Marilene dressed, and stepped out of the clinic, arm in arm, into bright spring sunshine and warmth. We were floating. I actually had the giddy sensation that I might not be able to keep my feet down on the sidewalk.

Try to convince an expecting parent at this moment that there is no magic. And good luck with that.

Impatience

Kevin's drive was apparent from the get-go. He arrived three weeks early, on July 31, 1998. Marilene had not so much as an aspirin for this—her first—birth, over a seven-hour labor.

The only drama we had during the labor was a moment when the nurse attending us burst into the room with another nurse in tow. She insisted that Marilene turn on her side immediately; something about the baby's heart rate being too low. Marilene and I were alarmed because the nurse behaved so frantically. But at that moment, cooler heads prevailed. Dr. Cunningham—an African- American gentleman and the doctor in charge—came into the room and calmly assessed the situation. The frazzled nurse at one point insisted on something. But Dr. Cunningham wasn't having it. He raised a flat hand in the "hold on" signal, and calmly, slowly but firmly said "Nooo, we're going to do this." At once, it was clear who was in charge, and the blood pressure of everyone in the room eased off.

The low heart rate turned out not to be as alarming as some thought, so that drama subsided, and we got back to work. As Marilene's contractions grew stronger, her breath caught up short each time. She has a very high pain tolerance, so I knew when she complained, the pain had to be intense. I deep-massaged her lower back, which seemed to ease her discomfort, if only a little. Maybe it just felt good to have the support.

Only seven hours after her water broke, the doctor told Marilene it was time to push. Marilene's face set in grim determination. I have since reflected on what this moment must have meant. She has immense strength, despite her small frame. She drew from that strength. She drew from the knowledge that her own mother had fourteen kids! Her family is *good* at this ! She drew from the confidence and composure of Dr. Cunningham. No doubt she drew from millennia of hormones, telling her, compelling her, that *this* was the time to bring her baby to her. And I'd like to think she drew strength from me, from the look in my eyes at her as she pushed.

Can something that happens thousands of times a day, all over the world, qualify as a miracle? Before this, I would have said no. It's part of the endless, winding chain of existence. But that was a different me. Now I know better. They all are. Miracles. Every single one.

Kevin weighed in at just under six pounds, small but not worryingly so for a baby that early.

Within minutes after his birth, I was with him in a newborn's room while the doctors and nurses helped Marilene recover. Kevin had the little fingers of his right hand wrapped around my right thumb, as I watched over him. I was surprised by the strength he showed even then, twenty minutes after he was born. His tiny thumb and fingers gripped my thumb tightly! I was quietly laughing, at the same time tearing up, with pride and delight.

The nurse came in and needed to give Kevin a vitamin K shot. My eyes grew to saucers when I saw the size of the hypo needle. *Jeez, don't they have a newborn size?!* I said to myself. She proceeded to bury that needle an inch deep into Kevin's little thigh. I remember thinking in alarm: *Damn! Are you trying to get it into bone or something?!* But my alarm was the only distress in the room. Not a peep came from Kevin. He gripped my thumb throughout.

Being born on July 31 made Kevin a Leo (the Lion) on the zodiac signs. He was whole, pink, handsome, and healthy. The only distinguishing mark on him was a red blotch-like birthmark on the lower left side of his back. It was shaped like the map of Peru, only turned ninety degrees clockwise.

Brazilian Viking Mormon

Tracing back not too far, Kevin's family tree is far from vanilla.

My father was Danish. He went to university during the years that the Nazis occupied Denmark. After earning his PhD in Scandinavian literature, he came to the US after World War II to pursue an academic career. He taught Scandinavian Studies and Drama at the University of California - Berkeley until his retirement. I felt for my father. He had the pangs of the displaced immigrant. I don't think he ever felt fully accepted in the US, at least not on his own terms. He didn't know American baseball or football, so could not teach me those things. Plus, the markers of status and prestige that he had strived for in Denmark simply meant less in the US. A few times, he let slip some murmurings of regret at the course he had taken in life.

That said, my father spoke four languages: Danish, English, French, and a fair bit of German, which he had absorbed during those years of Nazi occupation from 1940 - 1945. I remember him telling us stories of listening to the BBC radio, there in Denmark. The BBC was actually banned by the Germans, but people tuned it in on the sly. My father said that they used to huddle near the radio turned on low, and thrill to hear the exploits of George Patton as he raced across Europe in 1944-45, or to hear Winston Churchill's latest speech. My father would even mimic both Churchill *and* Hitler. He could perform snippets of a Hitler speech in German, with all the bile and animation of the original. So one gift my father gave me was that I never feared learning a new language.

My mother was American back several generations. She grew up in a Mormon family in Utah, but she never subscribed to Mormonism as an adult. Cool factoid up my mom's family tree: her great-grandfather was known as an even faster-draw than Wild Bill Hickok. My mom lost her father when she was just thirteen. Her mother was a stern sort and never permitted my mother or her older brother to express grief. So I think that unexpressed grief bottled in her for the rest of her life. Her mother didn't drive, so they appealed for and received driver's licenses for both my mother and her brother at younger ages than usually allowed. Years later, my mom started to teach me to drive a stick-shift on an old Volkswagen Beetle when I was just fourteen. My mother taught high school and later, college-level English.

I was born in 1956, followed by my sister Annalise in 1957 and our brother Peter in 1960.

We grew up in the East Bay area near San Francisco. We lived in a small suburban house on a hill in El Cerrito, just north of Berkeley. From the street in front of our house, we could look west, across the San Francisco Bay, and watch sunsets through the Golden Gate Bridge. On hot days, Dad welcomed the cooling fog which streamed over the San Francisco and Marin County hills and mountains and through the Golden Gate on its way east to us. Our elementary school was a block away; the local middle school (we called them junior high schools then) was a block and a half.

My father loved jazz. He had a collection of records which included Nat King Cole, Louis Armstrong, and Billie Holliday. When Louis Armstrong passed away, my father wept. My mom hated Billie Holliday, but I inherited my dad's love for this music and later passed some of that along to our kids.

We lived a somewhat cocooned suburban existence, as around us swirled all of the turbulence of the Sixties and Seventies: Vietnam; the Cold War; The Cuban Missile Crisis; the Free Speech Movement; the Civil Rights Act; hippies; drugs; the assassinations of JFK, MLK, and RFK; the sexual revolution; and Watergate. Looking back on it now, it reminds me of the old Chinese curse: *May you live in interesting times.* It was an interesting time to be a teenager.

Paraguassu Paradise

My wife Marilene comes from a small rural town in Brazil. Paraguassu, in the state of Minas Gerais, is one of my favorite places on Earth. Driving through the country in Minas, the landscape unfolds in mile after mile of rolling green hills. Iron-rich clay soil, a surprising rust-red, grows anything. Abundant dairy cattle support one of the country's largest cheese-producing industries. Coffee and corn are the main crops. Green is everywhere. A corn crop on one hill looks from a distance like a buzz-cut of light green. The hill on the other side of the road grows the deep, thick dark green of coffee, looking like cornrows from a distance. After a rain, the grass fields where the cattle graze sport an almost-neon green, the color of fresh moss on a moist tree trunk. And thick, outrageous bamboo stands—in a tangled, woven look, often forty feet tall—grow in the low areas between hills and fields.

Farm fields separate the towns, usually by several kilometers, and you share the road often with slow tractors or horse-drawn carts. These roads are typically two-lane, undivided highways, snaking around and between the hills. It is not unusual to spot a toucan flying over the road as you drive by, and you wonder how the thing flies with that long green-yellow beak out front. You would think the aerodynamics or the balance would be off. But it does fly, thank you very much, and even quite gracefully. And you count it as a good luck omen.

Marilene's town reminds me of a travel poster. Paraguassu drapes over a series of hills, its cobblestone streets climbing up and down and across. About 30,000 people live there, most of whom live in houses painted in white or pastels, with ceramic Spanish-style tile roofs. You're embedded in farm country, so you'll frequently see—and hear—horses in the town streets, clopping over the cobblestones. The town grew up around a central square (the *praça),* bordered on one side by the main town church with its steeple and bell-tower visible from miles away, the main reference-point for the entire area. Commerce surrounds the praça on its other three sides: a small, quaint hotel; various bars and restaurants, an ice cream shop that's been there for decades on the corner across from the church, a pharmacy, a *supermercado.* The streets which square the praça frame a park with trees, stone-paved walkways, a pond with fountains, and a gazebo where people gather, chat, play cards, or sometimes play instruments. People wave or honk, or simply stop in the street to talk, until traffic prompts them to move. Marilene tells the story of how her parents met. In the '40s, on a Saturday night, the girls would saunter around the praça sidewalk in twos or small groups, walking clockwise. The young men did the same, but in the other direction, counter-clockwise. Marilene's parents—Mozart and Maria de Lourdes—met there, in the middle of town at the praça, in 1942, performing an age-old ritual no doubt practiced in hundreds of similar small towns throughout Brazil. I can just picture a young, rakish Mozart chatting up a demure but charismatic Lourdes in the warm spring air. I love that story.

Another little story might help you feel the vitality of the town and the role of the praça at the center. Marilene and I passed the Christmas and New Year's holidays in Paraguassu in 1997-8, a year after we married. At about 10:30 p.m.on Christmas Eve, Marilene suggested we drive up to the praça. With my American sensibility, I thought that would be a waste. I said, "Why would we do that? It's almost midnight on Christmas Eve. There'll be no one there."

Marilene heard me, but said, "Oh, let's just go see."

So we went. It's a short drive from her folks' house up to town, maybe half a mile. I expected a darkened, fairly empty square. But I was about to get one of my first Brazilian culture shocks, and it was a good one.

A massive *festa (*party) blanketed the praça. Had you not known the date, you would have guessed New Year's Eve, not Christmas Eve. No less than two thousand people crowded there. People sat on the dozens of benches. Others walked, talked. Some cruised slowly around the square in their cars, speakers pumping Brazilian country music or club music. All the bars and restaurants were open, with people spilling out into the street. A few food stands operated at different spots near the square. Beer flowed in abundance, and the crowd was animated, festive.

As I drove and joined the cars cruising around the square with our windows down (Christmas is in summer south of the equator; it was quite warm, even at almost 11 p.m. Many wore flip-flops, shorts, and tee shirts or short sleeves), it seemed that every couple hundred feet someone shouted Marilene's name. A friend or friends would come up to the car, a happy reunion of sorts took place—in mid-cruise—and we agreed we would see them later for a beer (*cerveja)*. This happened maybe five times during one circuit of the square.

I love this place! I thought. *Where I come from, everything closes at night on Christmas Eve.*

Americans have a perception of Brazilian culture: laid-back, celebration, sun, warmth, music, samba, Carnival, living for today and for family and friends. Most Brazilians would embrace this characterization. The phrase in Portuguese which best captures it is *"Tudo bem,"* which translates roughly as "It's all good."

Tudo bem has its own little story:

Diego meets Bruno in the street. He greets him as usual: "Tudo bem, Bruno?"

Bruno replies: "Well, my wife left me, my dog died, and my house burned down." Pause. "But tudo bem."

We should all be a little more Brazilian. I am flattered to be as embraced by Marilene's family as I have been. When people now ask me, I tell them that I'm half Danish, half American, and three-quarters Brazilian. If you just did the math and said to yourself, "Hey, that adds up to more than 100%!" you're exactly making my point about the difference between Americans and Brazilians. But tudo bem.

The Prado Clan

Marilene was born Marilene Silva Prado, which in Portuguese is like saying "Marilene Smith-Jones." Silva and Prado are both proud Spanish and Portuguese surnames going back centuries. There's a town museum in Paraguassu, on a cobblestoned, tree-lined mini-praça adjacent to the original old blue church. The museum captures the history of the town with old farm implements and antique kitchen appliances and musical instruments, an old dentist's office, as well as with hundreds of captioned old photos, going back to when the town was established around 1900. In about half those photos, the captions list one, or more, or several Prados, and often some Silvas, as well. As I walked through the museum with Marilene, my eyes widened as she pointed out "Oh, that was my great-grandfather" or "That was my grandfather's sister," and so on. Only, when I say "so on," I mean that she pointed out *several dozen* relatives or ancestors. I—coming from a small family—began to appreciate the roots and the legacy of the family into which I had married. This legacy would be re-emphasized when we later visited the town cemetery. The way they bury people there is in above-ground, bricked-in mausoleums, mostly. Sometimes a whole family is buried in one mausoleum, its chambers filled, one by one, over forty or fifty years. I should not have been surprised, given what I had seen in the town museum, but about one in four mausoleums there has plaques with the names Prado or Silva.

Marilene is the youngest of fourteen siblings: eight girls; six boys. All were single births; no twins. Her mother, Maria de Lourdes (Lourdes) stayed pregnant basically between 1945 and 1965, with few breaks. Lourdes was raised devout Catholic, and a lady, educated in a French school near Paraguassu. And as a lady, she never, ever cursed. Marilene shared stories from her childhood, Lourdes burning herself at the stove, and exclaiming *"Bunda de gato!"* ("Cat butt!") That was about as salty as Lourdes ever got. Not only did she raise fourteen kids, Lourdes also taught grade school, including many if not most of her own children.

Marilene's father Mozart (Mozart Luiz do Prado) came from a line that had been among the first settlers in Paraguassu around 1900. In the 20th century, about a half dozen Prados were mayors of Paraguassu: Mozart was not one of those, but they were his relatives. Mozart grew up on a farm. He almost went to Europe in World War Two, but the Allies prevailed and celebrated V-E Day, so happily Mozart's deployment became unnecessary. Mozart got home just in time for the birth of his first child, Maria Elzira. Mozart and Lourdes (birth name Maria de Lourdes) thought it would be fun to give all their kids names which started with "M." So, in order: Maria Elzira, Marcilio, Marcel, Magda, Marco Antonio, Mariza, Maria Auxiliadora, Marcio, Martinho, Marcia, Maristela, Marina, Marlon, and finally, Marilene. Unfortunately, Maria Elzira passed from cancer in 1990, and Marcel just passed a few months ago in 2019. All the other siblings survive.

Whatever criticisms anyone might level at Mozart and Lourdes, one could never say that they didn't have a…zest for life.

Mozart tried various livelihoods. He loved to create, build, and was boldly—almost recklessly—entrepreneurial. He converted a car to run on home-made fuel once. He once owned a bar, and not just an everyday bar, but a fairly upscale one. Marilene told me once that Mozart had the only bottle of Dom Pérignon in the town. But that bottle was not for show, or promotion, or display. That Dom was consumed soon after it came to Paraguassu. At another point, Mozart used to buy and sell trees and plants. But I imagine that this was too much a commodity business for Mozart, even though he loved plants and trees. But the business which finally stuck and sustained the large family over decades and still sustains three sons, is the lumberyard and hardware store, Madeireira Paraguassu. Two or three concrete benches at the main praça are sponsored by Madeireira Paraguassu, and you can sun yourself on those benches and take in the bustle around the praça.

In stark contrast to the Brazilian side of the family, I grew up in California, the oldest of three kids. It's just a fact that Kevin and Gustavo have far more Brazilian family than American. They have more than thirty Brazilian aunts and uncles, more than forty cousins, and a similar number of nieces and nephews. In a family this large, you often have nieces or nephews older than their aunts and uncles. At Christmas 2017, Marilene's aunt Gislene (one of Mozart's sisters) brought a family tree in a parchment scroll that traced back to Mozart's father and forward to his children, *their* children, and *their* children. The scroll was three meters long. And that was just the father's side of the family; the mother's side is a project for another day.

Marilene

I met Marilene (MAH - ree - LEHN - ee) at her sister's wedding in 1990. My friend and work colleague Greg Dunn met his now-wife Maristela (Marilene's sister) while he was on assignment with Clorox in Brazil. I was able to go to Greg's Brazilian wedding by burning through some 80,000 miles on the old Pan Am Frequent Flier program, and I brought my good friend Eric Sagen along. We flew overnight from San Francisco to Miami and then from Miami to Rio de Janeiro. From Rio we hired a puddle-jumper airplane for the somewhat-hairy, bumpy flight to a small, packed-dirt airfield right there in Paraguassu.

At the Prado family home in Paraguassu, people converged from all over for the coming wedding. Eric and I were meeting dozens of people, fumbling all the names which started with "M," and I butchered the language with a crude attempt to blend my novice-level Spanish with the handful of Portuguese words I tried to pick up. We joke that I often speak (spoke) "*Portuñol*" (Portuguese + Español). Years later, Kevin and Gustavo never tired of critiquing my Portuguese, as they spoke it like the locals, like true Mineiros (natives of Minas Gerais).

As the wedding attendees gathered for the coming celebration, Marilene arrived at the house after most of the family, because she had a bit of a journey from another city she lived in at that time. I noticed her right away. She is petite—about five foot one. She has dark brown hair and dark brown eyes, arched with thick, expressive eyebrows. She beamed a joyous, ready smile for her loved ones, spoke animatedly, and had that twinkle in her eye. And yeah, I admired her toned brown legs, too. The room sparked when she arrived.

That twinkle in her eye was not initially directed at me. That came much later. In fact, my first attempts at chatting her up gave Marilene the impression that I was an arrogant American. In my own defense, all I asked her was if she had driven home to Paraguassu from the city she then lived in, which was a couple hours away. I was just trying to make conversation, on subjects simple enough to bridge the language barrier: she spoke little English; I spoke poor Portuñol. For her part, she felt it was arrogant and presumptuous that I thought all Brazilians owned cars. No, she had not driven from her city; she had taken the bus, and she wasn't going to be made to feel badly about it by anybody, least of all, you, you stuck-up gringo! She didn't actually *say* all that, but she has no poker face whatsoever, so I could tell she was *thinking* it.

So I crashed and burned, at least in 1990. But I had seen something. This petite lady was a firecracker. Fierce things come in small packages.

Sparks Fly

Between '90 and '95, Marilene and I each went off and did other things. She spent a year and a half in London. I spent a year-plus in Hong Kong, with Clorox. We each got engaged to other people. We each got unengaged.

We met again in '95, when Marilene was visiting the US with her mother, Lourdes. Lourdes had had a stroke some years before, which paralyzed much of her right side, so she needed a lot of support in order to make such a trip. Marilene traveled with her. She spent a few weeks in Scottsdale, where her sister Maristela was living with Greg and their two kids, Christopher and Bryan. Greg by then had left Clorox and was working for the Dial Corporation.

Of course, Marilene had made an impression on me five years before, at her sister's wedding, when her nonverbal cues had let me know she had thought me an arrogant American. Ah, a chance for redemption! So, hearing that Marilene and Lourdes planned to visit Greg and Maristela, I "arranged" to be in Scottsdale for several days. I had other business in and around Phoenix, so I stayed at a nearby hotel. But I visited Greg and Maristela one evening. I remember Marilene made me a *caipirinha* (a Brazilian version of the margarita but made with a different liqueur). As she handed me the drink in her sleeveless dress, I noted the sculpted tone in her bronzed upper arm.

After dinner at their house that evening, Marilene and I went out for drinks, and began to get to know each other. Of course, in Phoenix you can be outside at night. We went to a spot with an outdoor pool and fountains, cacti, and firepits. Since Marilene had spent a year and a half in London, she had improved her English dramatically, so we were much better able to talk than we had been able to back in 1990. I must have cracked the "arrogant" perception some. Anyway, a chemistry began to form.

On their next stop after Scottsdale on their trip to America, Lourdes and Marilene passed through the San Francisco Bay Area. How nice for me! I asked Marilene out for a proper dinner date, and she said yes.

Our courtship unfolded over the months of November 1995 to February 1996. By then, we were serious, and we began talking about her moving in with me, to my townhouse in Oakland. In February, she flew up and moved in.

I still marvel at the courage it took for Marilene to leave her life in Brazil and come to the US to be with me. I think she is far more courageous than I, or than almost anyone we know. She left her career as a practicing psychologist. She left her family, and as we've seen, that is a large family. She left all her friends, her first language, and her culture. In the US, when we moved in together, after some months she overstayed her tourist visa, so that put her at some risk.

This was the first time I had ever lived with someone. I was very happy we were together, but also after the sacrifices she had made, I took nothing for granted. She soon found work caring for the baby son of two attorneys, who lived not far from us in Oakland. This helped a lot, because before this, when I was at work, Marilene had had way too much idle time.

So from March to November, we both worked. We loved our morning ritual: coffee at Peet's in Montclair Village; I dropped her off at the babysitting job; then I went off to work at Clorox in downtown Oakland. We enjoyed nights out, especially at our favorite local spot, Italian Colors. We socialized with friends. We took weekend trips to various California spots of interest: the wine country, Mendocino, Carmel and Monterey.

In late November 1996 I booked a trip to Maui for the two of us. At dawn on December 4, at the top of the dormant volcano Haleakala, I asked Marilene to marry me. She was happy but didn't answer me right away. But by the time we had driven halfway down the mountain, and we stopped for breakfast along the way, she had said yes and that she would take on Madsen as her last name.

We married ten days later, in a simple ceremony at Lake Tahoe. Why the rush, after we got engaged? We needed to get her legal residence sorted out as quickly as possible. Remember, she had overstayed her tourist visa. So the sooner we married, the sooner we could file all the documents and sort out her legal status. We did a proper wedding party in Oakland in April 1997, catered by our friends at Italian Colors. That was followed soon after by a big party in Brazil, with all her family and friends.

Chile

After Kevin came onto the scene in July 1998, we lived and worked in Oakland for the next several months, as Kevin gained weight and took on personality. In April 1999, a position at Clorox's subsidiary in Chile opened up. I put my name in the hat, and Clorox said yes. So Clorox took us to Santiago in April 1999, when Kevin was less than a year old and Marilene was pregnant with Gustavo. During these four-plus years in Chile and later Argentina, we really tried to raise the boys tri-lingual. We were fortunate enough to have maids/nannies, so the boys got Spanish from them. Marilene tried to speak exclusively Portuguese with them. And I was almost their only source of English. For a while there, English was for sure their third language.

Kevin's first sentence was in Portuguese; *"Cade a lua?"* which means "Where is the moon?" which Marilene had been saying with him every night when they stepped outside. Marilene would also play the "I got your nose!" game with him, also in Portuguese, of course. That's the one where you pretend to pinch off someone's nose, then tuck your thumb between your fingers to show your partner, "See? I got it!" One day he pre-empted her, pinching her nose, tucking his thumb between his little fingers, and saying *"Pegue!"* ("I got it!")

One evening, at the house in Chile, Marilene came up to Kevin and said to him (in English, unusually for her, since she usually spoke Portuguese with him), "Kevin, you want to wash your hands?"

Kevin—just eighteen months old then—looked up at her, over to me briefly, then back to her, and said *"¿Lava manos?"*

Startled, I looked at Marilene, eyes wide and jaw dropped. "He just translated English to Spanish!"

Kevin seemed a happy and curious baby and toddler. Soon after we moved to Chile, but before Gustavo was born, Marilene and I went for dinner to a *barrio* in Santiago called Pio Nono. Pio Nono had been home to Pablo Neruda, the Nobel prize-winning Chilean poet, back in the '50s and '60s. These days, the area holds a number of upscale bars and restaurants, housed in buildings maintained true to the historical architectural style. On this dinner date, we brought Kevin along in his stroller. As we pushed the stroller along the sidewalk on one block, I picked up speed to entertain Kevin. He sat up straight, leaned slightly forward against the little seatbelt, and stretched his arms straight out to the sides. Of course, I then had to run with the stroller, to provide him some airspeed....He "flew" the entire block, never got tired of it.

In so many ways, that's my permanent image of Kevin: arms wide, flying through life.

Gustavo Arrives

When we learned that Marilene was pregnant again, just six months after Kevin was born, we began to dream and plan.

"I bet you want a daughter now, huh?" I started. "Since we already have Kevin?"

"No way!" Marilene insisted. "I want it to be another boy, so that the two of them can play together and be each other's best friends!"

That worked for me. I feared that had I been a father of a daughter, I would have been far too protective for her own good, and perhaps for the good of the father-daughter relationship.

And so it was. When we did the sonogram and learned that our new addition would be male, we were both ecstatic. Of course, we started discussing names. Since Kevin's was a European name, I wanted our next son to have a more Latin name. I preferred Gustavo, which is a common name in Latin America. It is also close to the Scandinavian Gustaf, so in a sense, it was a nod to my Danish roots. Marilene preferred other names; Adriano was one. I liked Adriano, but preferred Gustavo. I got my way on this one.

Gustavo came along in October 1999, six months into my work assignment in Chile. Marilene was attended by the doctors at the preferred hospital near us, the Clinica Las Condes. As opposed to the completely natural birth she had done with Kevin, we were a little put-out when we learned that the Chileans routinely gave birthing mothers epidurals, as well as episiotomies. We weren't thrilled with this, preferring the more natural approach for the sake of both mother and child. But another US expatriate mother helped us get over it when she said: "Yeah, that bothered me, too. But then I thought about it: Did I want to be the *only* one who did it differently than the way they were used to doing it?" Legitimate point.

Happily, Gustavo's delivery was pretty smooth. We brought Kevin— then fifteen months old—into the room where Marilene was recovering. Gustavo napped in a clear plexiglass bassinet, cushioned with blankets at the bottom, and Gustavo himself of course swaddled in the blue hospital blanket.

We explained to Kevin that this was his little brother. At this age, Kevin wasn't really speaking yet, at least not in sentences. I picked Kevin up and placed him on the bed next to the bassinet so he could get a closer look at his baby brother. At the same time, I was keenly vigilant, because I had heard stories of jealousy of newborn siblings, even physical aggressiveness against them. So as I placed Kevin on the bed near the bassinet, I hovered warily.

I need not have worried. As Kevin peered into the bassinet, Marilene and I cooed encouragement to Kevin. Kevin fixated on Gus, who remained asleep.

Slowly, as if he somehow knew he needed to be very careful, Kevin raised up and extended his right hand toward Gus's little face. Gus breathed peacefully, oblivious to all of this. Kevin gently brushed the back of his right index finger against his brother's pink cheek, then withdrew. It was a gesture of such caution and tenderness that we couldn't believe it of a fifteen-month-old. Looking back on it, I think that—even then—Kevin had some innate sense of being a big brother, and he wanted to do it right.

Santiago to Buenos Aires to Boston

From 2000 to 2003, my career with Clorox took us from Santiago, Chile, to Buenos Aires, Argentina. While in Buenos Aires, I left Clorox and joined the Gillette Company as their VP of Finance for the Latin America division.

During those years, Kevin grew from two to five years old. The boys went to Spanish-speaking pre-schools, honing their language skills. I remained their chief source of English.

In late 2003, Gillette decided to relocate its Latin America headquarters to Boston. So I - along with all the other executives and mid-level managers and their families - prepared for the move.

Natick

We bought a newly constructed house thirty minutes west of Boston, in Natick. Natick is immediately west of Wellesley, the town with the famous women's college. Natick was incorporated as a town in 1651. Some cemeteries there have headstones from the late 1600s. That's a couple hundred years more history than a Californian usually gets to see.

When I say "we bought" a house, it bears reading the fine print. Due to some heartburn or another with her green card, Marilene couldn't join me on the house-hunting trip. So I found the place, in a nice suburb, took a lot of pictures of the empty, newly built home, as well as pictures of the neighborhood and the upscale supermarket nearby. I shared all the photos with Marilene back in Buenos Aires. We agreed to pull the trigger and buy it, but I held my breath. Marilene is not the type to sit on a complaint, if she has one. Nor is a complaint a one-shot deal; it is the gift that keeps on giving.

Our first night in the new house in Natick, Marilene and I turned in, exhausted from the move-in. I said, "Good night" and began to drift off, lying on my left side. But just then, she draped her right arm over me, hugged me from behind and said, "Honey, I like the house."

Best words since "I do."

First Ski Trip

The mountains—such as they are—of New Hampshire are not the Rockies, nor the Sierras, but they were close enough to Natick that we could drive up there for the boys' first ski trip.

So we packed up the van and took the trek to a family-oriented ski resort about two hours away. Kevin was maybe six. After we got everyone bundled for the snow, and then rented our skis and poles, we set off. We took our first run off one of those platter, rope-tow ski lifts. Kevin, true to form, was ahead of us on the rope-tow. I thought we had made it clear that we would wait for each other at the top of the rope-tow, before setting off down the slope. Either Kevin never got that memo or he just disregarded it. He unhooked from the platter at the top of the rope-tow, managed to turn right to get to the top of the slope, and he went.

That is, he went straight down that slope. Now, anyone who's skied knows that rope-tow slopes are pretty lightweight. Usually they slope gradually, they're nicely groomed, with no real ruts or moguls to trouble unskilled skiers. And they have plenty of those...unskilled skiers. Rookies, little kids, teachers with groups often start them off on these slopes.

And when I say that Kevin went straight down that slope, I mean no turns, no attempts to stop, no falling onto his butt to bail out of his run. I don't know how he didn't collide with another skier. A small snowbank near the bottom of the lift finally collected him. He sprung back up, brushed the snow off, and headed for another run. This time I re-explained the concept of meeting together at the top before taking off.

Kevin's brother Gustavo, five at this time, was a much more cautious chap. Gustavo was afraid of falling or hitting something, as I was when I started skiing, and as I think most of us are. After several runs, Gus managed to slowly snowplow down the entire slope without falling. He plowed to a stop, triumphantly whacked his ski pole onto the snow and shouted, "Whoa, I'm a Level *Four*!" To this day I have no idea what that meant, but that was one bubble I wasn't about to burst.

Go West

In 2005, we received a news flash: Procter & Gamble was buying Gillette.

When large companies acquire other large companies, they try to harvest "synergies." To oversimplify, larger scale should make certain operations more efficient, able to operate with less overhead, saving money for the new, combined enterprise.

At Gillette, I was the Vice President of Finance for Latin American operations. Turned out that Procter & Gamble already had one of those. I met the guy and found him quite likable. I thought I was better than he was. But Procter is renowned for promoting its own. So I knew pretty soon that I was going to be a synergy.

But combining two multi-billion-dollar operations would take several months of planning, integration, and execution. So I had quite a bit of runway before I would need to depart Gillette/P&G. I began reconnecting with different executive-search firms, shaking the bushes, trying to cultivate my next opportunity.

A couple of flirtations went quite far down a path, with interviews in Miami, New York, Los Angeles, and Omaha, only to fizzle just shy of a job offer. As the months dragged on, I began to get antsy; no, I began to stress, actually.

I will never underestimate the importance of the role the spouse plays in such circumstances. I imagined some of my peers—also being displaced by the P&G acquisition of Gillette—getting squeezed by their wives, the closer their exit dates approached. Marilene never went there. Even as I got frustrated and anxious when a couple of promising opportunities went sideways at the eleventh hour, she remained steady. "Don't worry, sweetie," she said, more than once, as we lay in bed before going to sleep, "Something good is going to happen soon. Something even better for us is out there." As Jackie Gleason (playing bus driver Ralph Kramden) used to say to Alice on *The Honeymooners,* "Baby, you're the greatest!"

Finally, Marilene's prediction popped. Safeway Stores headquarters was seeking a VP of Finance, in Pleasanton, California. This would place us within fifteen miles of where we last lived in California. I ran the interview gauntlet successfully, joined Safeway in April of 2006, and lived in an apartment for two months while the boys finished their school year in Natick and Marilene geared up for the cross-country move.

So in June 2006, we headed west. We landed in the town of Danville, an hour east of San Francisco. Danville has a lively, charming town center, with upscale and atmospheric shops and restaurants. The school district earned the best scores in the area, and the development we landed in had a number of families with kids close in age to ours. It was a great spot to raise a family. Kevin was almost eight; Gustavo was six-and-a-half.

The house we bought, and would live in for ten years, had a pleasing curbside appeal. The home itself was pleasant, but not much updated. But the back yard sold us on the place. The back yard had a swimming pool with a broad waterfall and a heated jacuzzi, a gas grill with a granite outdoor bar, a half-court basketball set-up, a large trellis covered in wisteria, an outdoor pool table, and a gas fireplace with a seating area. We could see many parties in our future.

"This place is Club Med," I said to Marilene when we first visited the house.

I loved the house, and especially that back yard. But I eyed that waterfall a little warily. It was a built-up plateau made from numerous rough rocks, with broad, flat smooth rocks on top in a shallow stairstep scheme to allow the water to cascade down across a wide swath. The lip of the waterfall stood four feet over the surface of the water in the pool and stretched fifteen feet wide. It looked a little hairy to me, so I called the boys over.

"Listen, we will enjoy this back yard and this pool a lot. But there has to be one rule: No one climbs up there to jump off that waterfall! We clear on that?" I got the boys to acknowledge my order.

Three days later, I returned from work on a very hot day. I found Marilene in the kitchen. I heard noise in the back yard. Sounded like the boys were having fun.

Stepping through the sliding glass door which opened onto the back yard from the family room, I spied both Kevin and Gustavo, standing together at the lip of the waterfall, counting 1-2-3 before they both launched into the pool four feet below, seeing who could make the biggest splash. And oh yes, they were naked.

After they splashed, they swam back over to the rocks below the waterfall, scrambled back up to the top, selected their preferred launch-spots, and jumped again. Somewhere in there, I think I got a "Hi, Dad!" from the two of them. I stood there, hands on hips, glaring, but with a resigned curl to my lip, before stepping back into the kitchen.

Marilene stood there, looking at me, a guilty smirk on her face. She knew damn well what the rule was. I felt like Rodney Dangerfield: "I don't never get no respect!"

I peered out the window, where the two naked boys, seeming never to tire, leapt once more into the air, this time doing cannonballs.

"Yeah, this house'll do," I finally said.

Bedtime Stories

When we moved to Danville from Boston, the boys at first shared a large bedroom in which we staged twin beds. These were the years when Kevin would have been eight to eleven. At bedtime I read stories to them. *Goodnight, Moon* was a favorite, as was *Where the Wild Things Are*. There was this illustrated book on castles that we got a kick out of, too. It was full of knights and nobles, serfs and clergymen, construction and sieges, all in beautiful color illustrations. On one page it showed in cross-section a castle turret overlooking the moat. I used to tell the boys that the guards in the turrets would straddle holes in the stones at the top, in order to poop down into the moat. I made a whistling sound indicating that the turd was dropping like a bomb from the turret, and then a "plop" as it hit the water. The boys howled, every time. Even when we returned to that same page a week or so later, and they *knew* what was coming, maybe *because* they knew what was coming, the anticipation built, and the whistling, plopping turd doubled us all over again.

We had recycled the usual books several times, so one night I decided to make up a story with them, on the fly. I ginned up a story taking place five hundred years ago in Siena, Italy. The story was about the Palio, which is a famous and dangerous horse race through the center of Siena, in Tuscany. Siena goes back to medieval times, and the Palio likewise. Our hero was a young guy named Flavio, who was training a horse that would run in the Palio in a few weeks' time.

Over the evenings of a couple weeks, I would curl up in one of the twin beds with one of the boys. We alternated this, to be fair. One night I would curl up with Kevin, the next night Gustavo. In truth, it was easier to pair up with Gustavo, because Kevin was larger, and these twin beds were tough to fit two. Then, we would first have to recall where we'd left off with the Palio story the night before. We turned this into a bit of a game. The boys each took pride if they could be the first to remember where we'd left Flavio. Kevin was spooky good at this. He always had the best memory in the family. Once we'd agreed where we'd left off the night before, I had to pick it up from there.

This wasn't easy. I really made all of it up on the fly. Somehow, I managed to generate some suspense and intrigue with Flavio. At first, he was simply a horse trainer for some noble or other. But along the way, some misfortune sidelined the noble, and Flavio would need to ride in the race. This seems like a thrill at first glance, but I made clear that it was a decision not to be taken lightly. The Palio carried a lucrative purse for the winner, and maybe more important the winner became an instant celebrity and earned bragging rights for his *contrada* (roughly, a neighborhood; each contrada is represented by a flag and a coat-of-arms, most with some bird or animal on them: a snail, a goose, a panther). The *contrade* also run back several hundred years in Siena. But while the Palio offered attractive rewards, it carried huge risks, as well. Riders were often maimed or killed, accidentally or...I hinted...otherwise...!

The contrade are hugely competitive about the Palio and have been for centuries, so I could weave into the story spying, sabotage, and bribery. Of course I inserted much about Italian life and food as I imagined it in the 1500s. And I had to include a love-interest for Flavio. So he gets a crush on a girl from another—vengeful—contrada.

Once I began the story, it flowed. It seemed to tell itself sometimes, through me. Many nights, the boys and I would fall asleep together. That made it tough to pick up the thread the next night. But we always managed. And I never knew where the story would go the next night. I let it take me where it wanted to go.

Of course, Flavio competes in the Palio. Despite all the dangers and attempts to sabotage him and his horse, he fends off all setbacks and wins. As the victorious hero, he gets carried off on the shoulders of his fellow contrada mates. And he gets the girl, too. They have kids. And he trains them to ride, as well.

The boys loved this story. I looked forward to telling it each night. I think Marilene listened secretly some nights, just out of sight around the door jamb.

I wish I had made up more stories with the boys at that age.

Rock City

Mount Diablo—at almost 4,000 feet—overlooks the valley which includes the Town of Danville, where we lived from 2006 - 2018. It (Mt. Diablo) is a regional park, so it is now protected from development. Not far from the summit of Mount Diablo is a popular site called Rock City. Rock City has dozens of acres of mostly glacier-smoothed boulders, canyons, arroyos, and even a few small caves. Any Cub Scout within a twenty-mile radius has visited Rock City, trust me.

When Kevin was ten, on one such Cub Scout outing, we and a few other parents took him and a number of the scouts from his "den" up to Rock City. That day just sparkled. The warmth on our shoulders and the crisp light made all things sharper, as if all around us was dialed up to a slightly higher energy level and you could pick it up in the hairs on the back of your arms. You felt that time gave you a nod and slowed for you. You felt beyond awake.

The boys bounded over the boulders, Kevin most of all—effortless, confident, fearless. His friends followed, but they moved more deliberately, step-by-step, as most of us would. For them, especially in the steep stuff, it was thought, step, grip, balance, thought, step, repeat. They moved in a staccato series of discrete steps.

In contrast with his friends, Kevin moved with fluid, animal grace. I thought of a puma. *He must be able to see several steps ahead*, I thought to myself. With him, you couldn't separate one movement from the next. He just moved in a flow, a continuum, without hesitation.

At one spot in Rock City, two granite slabs formed an eighty-foot-long, steeply inclined trough, shaped like a vee. The sides of the vee were too steep to climb, and smooth, not offering much in the way of handholds or footholds. At the top of the vee, the sides of the trough were about fifteen feet apart. I and a few of the kids paused at the bottom of this vee-trough, wanting to climb it but not sure at first how. It was quite steep, and a slip would for sure yield some serious road-rash.

Kevin strode through the few of us assembled there, and—characteristically, without pausing—sprinted up that trough by using the sides of the vee as foot-plants, alternating left-right-left-right, straight up to the top. Stopping would not have been an option; to stop would have been to fall. I and the others assembled at the bottom just marveled. One of his den-mates said "Hey, Kevin. That was pretty cool!"

I noticed that when Kevin climbed up or bounded over boulders, the adults in the group stopped talking. You couldn't maintain a thought sufficiently to carry on the successful back-and-forth of the conversation. You had to shut up and watch. At first, this was sheer parental concern. They all thought he was too reckless and would fall and hurt himself. After a while, though, we could all see that we were watching something rare. In the moment, you're just awe-struck. Later, on reflection, you might realize what it was that so compelled your attention. You had seen pure, unselfconscious joy and harmony.

Pinewood Derby

During 2008 - 2011, Kevin and Gustavo participated in Cub Scouts. Of course the reality is that when your kid joins Cub Scouts, so do you. You hold den meetings, you go camping, you organize Pack meetings, sell popcorn to raise money for local and national Cub Scouts, and help your son with his Achievements, which range from knot-tying to bicycle tire changing to birdhouse building to community service.

We thoroughly enjoyed the camping trips, most of them to Yosemite, and the long hikes in stunning natural beauty. And we did have some fun with the different Achievements and den and Pack meetings. But I think the event I most enjoyed, and the one which forged the tightest father-son bonds, was the Pinewood Derby.

For the uninitiated, The Pinewood Derby is a Cub Scout tradition, stretching back at least fifty years, I'm sure. The boys race wooden cars down an inclined track, propelled only by gravity. They all start with identical kits, which consist of a standard-size pine block, a set of four nails, four black hard plastic wheels, and some standard decals, like lightning bolts and racing stripes. From these basics, and working with their fathers, the boys build a car. On race day, the cars get released in groups of four to six, down a sloped polished wooden six-lane track. In a Cub Scout Pack of fifty scouts, an entire Saturday morning can get consumed as each car runs in a series of heats and races, with eventual eliminations, to arrive finally at the ultimate Pack winner. In addition to the Pack race winner, the judges (usually the parents of former Cub Scouts) award trophies for winners at each year level of Cub Scouts (there are four levels of Cub Scout, based on age). And then there are the aesthetic awards, for things like Most Realistic, Most Creative, Best Design, and so on.

In his last year as a Cub Scout, when he was twelve, Kevin and I sat down to plan and design his Pinewood Derby car.

"So, what's it gonna be, buddy?" I asked. "What do you wanna do for your car? We should make it special, because this will be the last one we do."

Kevin stared off, looking pensive. "Hmmmm...a super-hero car?" he began to brainstorm. "A stock car race car? A *Star Wars*-themed one?"

I tried to roll with Kevin's flow. "An *Indiana Jones*-themed one?" I offered. "A sports-team- themed one?" The brainstorming went on for several minutes. Some ideas just didn't grab us; others we liked but decided might be too difficult to build.

"Hey, wait!" Kevin jumped up. "I got it! How about the *Red October*?!*"

We had recently seen the movie *Hunt for Red October,* which was based on the Tom Clancy novel of the same name, about a high-tech Soviet submarine which defects to the US. Kevin and I both always sparked to those Tom Clancy movies. Once he suggested it, in a flash I imagined how we might build such a car from the requisite pine block and the regulation parts. At a glance, I didn't think it would be too hard to pull off.

"That's a great idea!" I enthused. "Let's do it!"

The Derby was about a week away. Over the next several nights, we set about cutting the pine block into the roughly torpedo-shape of a submarine and sanding it smooth. We added the conning tower by taking one of the cut pieces of pine and smoothing and sanding that into the proper shape, then gluing it to the top of our submarine. In a similar way, we cut vertical and horizontal tailfins from excess pine, and then fixed them into the tail into slots we cut there. We mounted a small propeller onto a nail and tapped that into the back of the submarine. And we even cannibalized a Lego *Star Wars* kit for some pieces we could glue onto the conning tower as the two horizontal fins or vanes on either side of it. After several hours of sanding, we painted the whole thing naval gray, three coats. And to finish off the cosmetics, we got two red star decals, and fixed them to either side of the conning tower.

We stepped back and admired our *Red October.*

"If we don't win the Best-Looking Award," Kevin began, "then there is no justice!"

I laughed and agreed with him. "It *does* look pretty cool, doesn't it?"

But we were not nearly done. We still had to do the wheels.

There is a lot of science to this. It's sad in a way, but you can find forty-page white papers online about how to build the fastest Pinewood Derby cars. These poor bastards with too much time on their hands even go into physics and cite geometric formulas on how and why you build them a certain way. Sadder still are the dads who actually read these white papers through, or even read several white papers before building their son's cars. In our competitive neighborhood, a handful of fathers took the Derby entirely too seriously, in my humble opinion. One of them— Seth Steele, a perennial front-runner and previous Pack winner—once admitted to me that he put in twelve hours on his son's car; there was no pretense nor shame that his son had done little or nothing on it. I chided him a bit: "Hey, isn't that *last* year's car, with a new paint job?" It looked identical to the one he had brought the last three years. Seth assured me he had built this one from scratch. Of course, Seth was not the only dad who soloed on his son's Derby car; there were at least three other dads who did the same, and predictably, those cars were always the fastest.

So in Kevin's last year of Cub Scouts, we knew the drill. We knew the same set of fathers would invest a week of their evenings building the slickest, fastest cars. Neither Kevin nor I wanted to invest twelve hours in building his car. We wanted to build a cool-looking car, and we wanted it to be competitive, if not the Pack-winning entry. To be competitive, we had to invest some labor in getting the wheels right.

Pinewood Derby winners usually turn out to be He Who Reduces Friction the Most. So you try like mad to minimize friction, or touchpoints, and where you must have touchpoints, you lubricate the hell out of them. This mantra forces some amazing attention to detail. The little nails which function as axles for the plastic wheels have small "nibs" on them, small projections of metal just under the nail head which attach down onto the shaft of the nail. Those nibs can cause the wheels to turn a little less freely, so they had to go. Kevin and I set about grinding them down with an electric drill with a firm round steel brush affixed. We would trade roles; sometimes he ran our "grinder" while I held a nail steady in a pair of pliers, then we would switch places.

After twenty or so minutes on each of four nails, we had ground down the nibs to our satisfaction, fingering them closely to be sure the projecting nibs were ground down and the entirety of the nail shaft was smooth. Next, we buffed down the outsides of the wheels to absolute smoothness with another attachment to our drill. Now it was time to attach the wheels and lubricate them.

"Lubricate" sounds like oil, but oil is prohibited at Pinewood Derby; it would make a mess. But graphite powder is permitted; it's dry, and is a very effective lubricant. We tapped each wheel into place, fed graphite powder into each axle, and spun the wheels to promote graphite coverage over the entire nail and onto the interior of the hole in the wheel. We also polished the outside of the wheels with graphite (since we had seen in years past that the "players" did the same). We tested our efforts by spinning each wheel, one at a time. A good wheel is one which spins freely and without shimmy for sixty seconds or more. If a wheel came up at only 45 seconds, you fed more graphite into the hole, and spun again, repeating until you got the result you needed.

Finally, after four nights—some until after midnight—of sawing, sanding, gluing, painting, measuring, buffing, and graphiting, Kevin and I pronounced *Red October* ready for competition. We looked at our creation, then at each other, with satisfied smiles. "This is the best one we ever built, Dad," said Kevin. Then we carefully placed the car into a shoebox lined with tissue, for transport the next day to the event.

Our Cub Scout Pack's annual Pinewood Derby event was held one select Saturday in the elementary school's Multipurpose Room, which doubles as the cafeteria during the week. Stalwart volunteers start at 7 a.m., trucking in and constructing the competition arena, with all its support scaffolding, electronic timing lights and stop-action video recorders at the finish line (yes, you read that right), and the smooth, polished wooden six-lane track, which at seven meters long must be fitted together piece by piece. Other volunteers show up soon with the donuts and coffee, yet others set up the folding tables to check-in the cars, others to display the cars for judging. Nowhere is the saying "It Takes a Village" more manifest than in Danville.

Kevin and I checked in *Red October,* after which it was staged on a display table with the other entries so the judges could review them all for the aesthetic awards. We stealthily surveyed our competition: I over the rim of my paper coffee cup, Kevin over his hot chocolate. There were some impressive entries, to be sure. But we felt good; very little looked like competition for *Red October,* at least for one or two of the aesthetic award categories.

As the time window for registration and weigh-in drew to a close, we saw a number of first-year Scouts and their dads file in. These weren't hard to spot. They had the youngest Scouts, of course. But the real "tells" were the disheveled, unshaven dads who shepherded their boys and their cars up to the registration table. These guys tried to slap a car together the night before, or even the morning *of.* They hadn't known how much was involved, and that you needed to start this project a week before the Derby. So we knew the look. Hell, I had *been* one of those guys just three years before. Many of these first-year dads got caught out at the weigh-in station. You see, among the rules of Pinewood Derby, a critical one is that the car must weigh no more than five ounces. Many of the rookies don't know about this, even though it's clear enough there in the directions (I can say that *now*). Their cars weigh in too heavy, and they are told to take it over to a fix-it station. The fact that something isn't right doesn't escape their young sons, who follow their dads in fear that their car will be somehow disqualified. So the dads—with a bit of a deer-in-the-headlights look in their eyes—hustle over to the fix-it station. If they're lucky, a veteran will be there to guide them. Then you'll see them desperately drilling holes into their son's car to lighten it, blowing the sawdust out of the holes, drilling some more, followed by several return trips to the electronic scale before the car makes weight and the sons—now relieved that they'll be able to race—run off in search of a donut and hot chocolate. Their dads by then look like they could use a hip flask.

The Derby runs the heats for the cars of the youngest Scouts first. So Kevin, being a senior Scout, had time to kill before any of his heats. He sought out his friends, to socialize. I did likewise with some of the parents. Finally, after ninety minutes, Kevin's first heat arrived. It takes time because—for fairness—each car gets to run in each lane of the track; that way, any lane variations should be averaged out in the race results. *Red October* placed second in Heat 1, finishing a fraction behind the winner. But we won Heat 2, Kevin and I high-fiving each other. We had a little validation and reward for all the hours put in, all the graphite we had used, and which stained our hands even that morning. Kevin was beaming. The car went on to place second in Heat 3, and third in Heat 4. Those results were strong enough to permit the car to go on to the Elimination heats.

In the Elimination heats, Kevin's car was up against stronger competition from winners of other preliminary heats, including one of the "ringer" cars. *Red October* fought valiantly and could rightly lay claim to "best of the rest, not-exclusively-built-by-dad" entries, but couldn't finish strongly enough to go on to the championship rounds. So our car's racing days were done. But this outcome had not been unexpected, really. We awaited news on the aesthetic trophy awards.

The judges completed their sweeps, and *Red October* was awarded Second Place Most Realistic. Kevin and I went to find the First Place Most Realistic entry. It was a crude red fire truck.

"You gotta be *kidding* me!" Kevin complained. "*That* is more realistic than *Red October*?!" I had to agree with him.

"You're right, son," I consoled. "Yours blows the doors offa that one! Whatever the judges think, you and I know that *Red October* is the most-impressive looking car here."

When the day's races and awards were done, about 1:00 p.m., we carefully re-packed *Red October* back into the shoebox with the tissue liner, along with our 2nd Place Most Realistic trophy, and shuttled back home.

Red October found a prominent home displayed on the top of Kevin's dresser.

Seven years later, Kevin was nineteen and we were packing his bedroom things to transport them to the dorm he would inhabit at St. Mary's College. *Red October* still kept its place of honor on his dresser, one of the few relics remaining from his younger years. I picked it up. Kevin, lying on his bed, set aside his phone and looked up. I gave him a knowing look and spun the left front wheel of *Red October*, counting, "One, one-thousand; two, one-thousand; three, one-thousand…." The wheel still spun surprisingly well, after all those years. I got to forty-five seconds before it finally wound down to a stop. "Not too shabby, son." Kevin returned a satisfied grin.

Maui

In 2012, in the space of a few months, we took our family on a couple of wonderful trips. One was to Europe; the second was to Maui.

Marilene and I wanted to take the boys on some memorable trips in that critical age-window between the ages of eleven and fifteen, when they would be old enough to appreciate things but not so old that it was no longer cool to hang with the parents. And - as to Maui - we also wanted to show them where we got engaged.

We spent four days, soaking up sun and beach and sights, swimming in the warm waters, and enjoying the local restaurants.

One evening in Maui I made reservations at Mama's Fish House. When in Maui, you must go. But you must have reservations. Mama's menu is different every day, based on the freshest fish they can acquire. So you'll see items on the menu like "Papio caught in deep sea reefs off Olowalu at 6 a.m. by Steven Kim Miyaki." It's expensive. In fact, it's very expensive, with entrees often over $50. But it's worth it.

I am nostalgic for Mama's. I first went there on a trip I took with my mother to Maui in the late '80s. Someone at the hotel pool recommended it. In fact, they said they had gone two nights before and they were going *again.* That kind of endorsement gets my attention. Mom and I went and had one of those meals that just surprises you and makes you feel like you hit a minor jackpot on the lottery. Later, in 1996, Marilene and I got engaged on Maui, at dawn on the top of Haleakala, the dormant volcano. We visited Mama's right after we got engaged. Another memorable meal.

Mama's is on the other side of Maui from Ka'anapali, about a 40-minute drive. So we collected up the boys, piled into the rental car, and off to Mama's we went.

The drive of course hugs the Maui coast. The sun was getting low, so the light reflected off the ocean as we cruised past the beaches, surfers, and palm trees. As I drove, I tuned the car radio. When I got to a reggae station, I tuned it in.

"You know," I said, "I don't usually listen to reggae, but somehow when I'm here in the tropics, it seems wrong *not to* listen to reggae." The relaxed, lilting beat resonates perfectly with the sensual pace of island life.

Mama's is open-air, because, well...it *can* be. It's Tiki-themed, with grass roofs, outrigger canoes hung from the rafters above, antique collector surfer posters and beach paintings, and native wood carvings, maritime relics, all done very tastefully, not kitschy. The restaurant is built just off of a beach on the northeast side of Maui. Small waves break on the beach, the rhythmic *shushhhhhh* sounds soothing the diners, on honeymoons, anniversaries, sipping exotic and top-notch cocktails. The only thing missing from your idyllic island experience is the sunset; since you're on the east side of the island, you miss that. But that loss may be the difference between $50 entrees and $70 entrees!

The four of us got seated at a cozy table fifteen feet from the sand, well within earshot of the breaking waves another two hundred feet away, and the sound of the breeze through the palm trees closer by. At Mama's, you simply cannot resist surveying the drinks and dishes being served all around you. You even ask other diners what they're drinking or eating, because what they have looks so good you just have to ask. And somehow it's not a breach of etiquette here, because that etiquette doesn't exist here, and even the people not from here seem to know right away that it's okay, because you're at Mama's and it's a shared experience.

The boys' eyes widened when they surveyed the menu and noticed the prices. I said, "Don't sweat it, boys. Order whatever you want. Special occasion."

They glanced at each other, each expecting his brother to figure out what special occasion they forgot. After a few seconds of blank stares, Gustavo asked, "What's the special occasion, Dad?"

"Well, we're in Maui, Mom and I got engaged at the top of this island, and Kev's birthday is in six weeks. Good enough?"

Now liberated, the boys returned to their menus with renewed interest and freedom. Kevin, who doesn't even like fish, chose the local *ono,* caught that day by Victor Wong off Hana, or something.

Following the melt-in-your-mouth fish, served in impossible sauces, we opted for dessert and even after-dinner drinks. Over dinner, we told stories and jokes. The smiles were more than on our faces. We all hummed to the same joyous frequency. After dinner, we took a walk on the beach.

Any family can name a handful of memorable meals, ticking them off on their fingers. For our family, this first one for us at Mama's Fish House, in Paia, Maui, is marked in stone.

D.C.

In 2013, we decided as a family to take a trip to Washington, D.C. We chose March, in the hopes of a nice spring and seeing the cherry trees in bloom.

Our flight arrived late, so we got to our hotel a couple blocks off the Mall at about 10 p.m. We could have decided to just turn in and go to bed, but having napped on the flight, none of us was sleepy. So I said, "Let's go for a walk. It'll help us sleep later."

Unusual for our family, I got no resistance to this idea. It was cold outside—temperatures in the 40s, but clear—so we bundled and layered, and off we went.

Crossing over a couple of blocks to the Mall, off to the west in the distance we could see the Lincoln Memorial, lit up at night. We walked briskly in that direction to keep the cold at bay, the boys often sprinting ahead as boys will do, playing tag with each other, or popping out to try to startle me and Marilene as we approached. As we neared the Memorial, we saw very few people; perhaps not surprising, given the hour and the cold. Climbing the steps, entering the memorial chamber eyes upward, we felt compelled to whisper. Only two other people shared the chamber with us.

I gazed for some minutes at the statue of the seated Lincoln. How—in stone—to have captured this?

Lincoln's gaze is levelled out through the columns and over the Reflecting Pool, sober, head inclined slightly forward, appearing deep in thought. The President's lanky frame fills the marble chair. His right hand is draped over the arm of his chair, the fingers of that hand loosely clutching the arm's edge, the index finger ever so slightly raised, as if he is formulating a sentence in his mind. His left wrist rests on the end of the other arm of the chair, leaving his left hand to project slightly out. The left thumb points forward, the knuckles of that hand half-closed, as if an invisible slip of paper is held between thumb and curved index finger, or he has just made a point on deeply held principle, on which he will not be moved. I stared for several minutes more. His gaze, his posture, the set and expressiveness of his hands, all combined to weight the air in the chamber with a permanent sense of loneliness, underpinned by fierce resolve.

We started back in the direction of our hotel but took a slightly different route, steering near the Tidal Basin. Across the waters of the basin one can see the Jefferson Memorial; it, too, was well-lit at night. As we crossed the paths and drew closer to the Tidal Basin, we noticed a structure on the shore, not far from us. It looked like a giant boulder, but it had to be man-made, because it was perfectly cleaved down the middle, a pathway ten or more feet wide cut between the two halves which rose in perfect vertical smoothness on either side of the opening. The opening was somewhat eerily lit from some stark, bright light behind and beyond the split boulder. It all felt slightly like a scene from *Close Encounters of the Third Kind,* but of course we had to know what was beyond, so on we walked.

Stepping through the opening, we could see beyond the first object *another* structure maybe eighty or a hundred feet away, looking like it was the missing piece from the large "boulder" through which we had just passed. It was about thirty feet tall, with smooth vertical sides. Bright spotlights shone on this object from the far side, near the shore. Ah, the main attraction!

Walking finally around to the front of the object, we stared up at the image of Dr. Martin Luther King, Junior, cut in stone. He wears a suit, his arms folded across his chest. His eyes reach out across the water, his expression measured, determined. The moment commands silence, contemplation. How do we not recognize greatness as it happens? Why does time magnify legend? Can he, wherever he is, feel my awe, my respect? Does my guilt matter? In the bright light, at night, and with no one else around, we felt privileged with our "exclusive" audience.

I tried to place myself in the minds of Kevin and Gustavo. What did this night mean to you, boys? What of the aura of these great men might seep into your pores, even a little? What curiosity may have been triggered in you, looking up at the faces of men so esteemed, not just here, but world-wide? If you've absorbed even a fraction of the wonder that I feel in this moment, and how happy I am that we've shared it together as a family, then maybe the payoff is that you're back here in thirty years, late on a cold March night with *your* family and children, looking up into the faces of Lincoln and King, remembering the wonder you felt then, and your children see in your eyes the same look that I'm giving you now.

We hustled back to the hotel then. We had been out for an hour and a half, we were getting colder, and it was around midnight. We slept well, after our night excursion. We passed another three good days in DC, visiting various museums, the Capitol, and several nice bars and restaurants. But nothing compared with those first few hours—alone as a family—on the first night we arrived.

Rugby

Rugby brought out the warrior in Kevin. He took up the sport at fifteen.

We didn't know the rules, but we thrilled to the rawness of it: its speed, strength, and power played out on grass, dirt and mud, non-stop. It's a festival of aggression, a test of wills and physical power. But once a match is completed, no matter how physically the match had played out, the teams form a circle in the center of the pitch (that's the field) and each team names a member from the opposing team as their "Man (or Woman; there are now Women's teams, too) of the Match." After all of that, adult teams go have a beer together. What a blend of aggression, nobility, and community! We loved it right away, even though the rules mystified us.

Kevin had always had natural strength and speed. Rugby seemed a great fit. And he had some schoolmates on the local club rugby team, the Danville Oaks. They told me that the Danville Oaks had 400 members, including female teams, and that they were the #1 club team in the country, in terms of size and tournament wins. Some of the coaches were South Pacific islanders, from places like Samoa and Tonga, where rugby is the number-one sport. One such coach was Tuggy Makaiwi. We loved Tuggy. He took Kevin under his wing, encouraged him, made him feel like a strong player and a valued teammate.

As most of us would be, learning a new sport, Kevin was a bit tentative the first several games. When the oblong ball spiraled over to him, Kevin would glance upfield, but then look to his side to pass the ball off to one of his teammates. He seemed reluctant to try to run with the ball himself. I—standing on the sidelines—could hear Tuggy and some of the other parents egging Kevin on to keep the ball and run with it sometimes. But he always dished it off, those first five or six games.

Around Game 7, I drove Kevin up to a match in Vallejo. On the drive up, after a pause in the conversation, I said to Kevin, "You know, dude, you can try and run with the ball. You know you're strong and fast. I guarantee you no one is going to be able to arm-tackle ya." Usually, such a suggestion from Dad would generate a retort from Kevin, saying I didn't understand the sport, there was a reason he always dished the ball off, or some other reason why he knew more than I did. I suppose it's the right of all teenagers to know more than their parents. But this time Kevin did not retort. He murmured some curt acknowledgement, but in a way that told me that I had at least got him thinking.

The match began as most had. When Kevin got the ball, he looked up field, but quickly then looked to his side and passed off to a teammate. I pictured a tense chat in the car on the ride home.

But about twenty minutes in, something happened. The Oaks were deep in their own end of the field, with the ball on offense. I stood on the sideline, along with other parents and coaches. The team was attacking from my left to my right. As one play unfolded, Kevin received a pass from a teammate, not far from where I stood. But this time, rather than the token glance upfield before looking off to his right to dish off, I saw

Kevin look upfield with a glint in his eyes, and his lips stretched back over his teeth, as if he would snarl. *Whoa!* I thought in that split second. Not looking to either side now, Kevin dug in his cleats, torqued his body out of lateral movement, hunkered low for power, and lunged upfield for turf. Protecting the ball as he weaved, he ran through one flailing tackle attempt after another, breaking through six tackles, for thirty yards upfield before he was stopped. I heard shouts of approval from Tuggy and several parents, all of us who had awaited this breakthrough. During the rest of the match, Kevin, having tasted some success running the ball, ran with it several other times, and scored a "try" (like a touchdown) late in that game. The Oaks won the match, too.

Walking off the field after the match, Kevin was greeted by Tuggy, who offered words of encouragement and a clap on the back. Tuggy glanced over at me and winked as they parted. I acknowledged him with a thumbs-up and waved "so long." As Kevin and I walked out to the parking lot, my chest swelling with pride, I said "Dude, you were a fucking *warrior* out there today! See what happens with a little channeled aggression?"

"Thanks, Dad." Kevin was often a man of few words. But I could feel his pride and he carried himself with an air of accomplishment. He finally knew he belonged on this team.

That car ride home was pure joy in testosterone.

Football

We always raised Kevin and his brother Gustavo under the mantra of "Never Look Back and Say 'I Wish I Would Have....'." It is far better to try, fail, and learn from it than never to try. We wanted the boys not to suffer the regrets of things not tried. As we approached Kevin's high school years, I was presented with the stark consequences of my own principle.

Kevin was desperate to play high school football. He had always been preternaturally strong, fast, and athletic. We had no doubt he had the raw materials to do well. But in 2014, the American public had been hearing concerns about concussions in football and other contact sports. It would all bloom fully into the public consciousness in 2015 with the release of the Will Smith movie *Concussion*. But it was already a big concern in 2014. The San Ramon Valley High School Football program enrollment suffered a drop of 40-50% that year, as parents steered their kids to other sports.

Had you asked me twelve or eighteen months before, I would have been certain and adamant: No way was Kevin going to play football. Too dangerous. But in that summer before his freshman year at SRVHS, I was confronted by my own principle: "Never Look Back and Say 'I Wish I Would Have.'"

If we had denied Kevin the opportunity to play football, as strong and as fast as he was, he would always wonder if he could have, and would always wonder how good he would have been. Strike One. Plus, Kevin would resent me/us for having prevented him from playing, probably for years. Strike Two. Plus, Kevin was getting to the age where we wanted him to make more decisions for himself. Strike Three. We did not question the social and confidence-building benefits of football, and we felt that Kevin needed some boost in confidence as he transitioned from middle school to high school. Strike Four. Heaven forbid that my own kid would throw my own principle back at me. Strike Five. Lastly, Kevin had something to *prove*. Strike Six, and maybe the most compelling of them all.

I remember the night that I realized that we were going to have to allow Kevin to make this decision for himself. I had shared the stories about the impact of concussions with him. He understood the risks. But that night, as Marilene and I went to bed, I said to her: "Son of a *bitch*, honey! We have to let him make this decision, or we're hypocrites about our own principles!"

And so, he played. He played at linebacker, defensive end, and offensive tackle, and even a little at tight end in pre-season scrimmages. In a number of games in his sophomore year, when he played on the school's junior varsity squad, Kevin played 85-90% of the time, as he started at both offensive line and defensive line. At the Awards Banquet in 2014, Kevin received the Coaches Award, recognizing him as the most-coachable kid on the Junior Varsity.

In the three years he played (he missed one year due to chemo and surgery), Kevin never missed a practice. Not only did he not miss a practice, he never once *complained* about practice. Kevin showed a depth of determination that I did not know he possessed before this.

Of course, the true test of physical strength, stamina, and mental toughness awaits all of the players...on the field, in a game, when it matters. I could share a number of examples of Kevin's accomplishments, but one stands out.

In his freshman year, San Ramon Valley faced Pittsburg High. Pittsburg had one of the stronger football programs in the area, so this was a match-up with some build-up beforehand.

As the teams lined up on the field after Pittsburg received the kick-off, I saw that Kevin—at right defensive end—was lined up against a much larger kid. Kev was about five feet, ten inches tall at this time, and weighed in at 175 pounds. But the kid opposite Kevin had to be at least six feet, two inches and not less than 210 or 220 pounds! I grimaced, expecting a "long day at the office" for Kevin.

But if Kevin was supposed to be cowed or intimidated by this huge opponent, maybe he was the only one who failed to get the memo. On Pittsburg's first play from scrimmage, their center snapped the ball to the quarterback, who handed off to a running back on his right side. To my surprise, Kevin stood up the much larger guy in front of him, forced him back into his own backfield, and contained the play from that side of the field.

That whole game, Kevin consistently forced his man back, disrupting Pittsburg's efforts on that side. Pittsburg attempted one run to that side, which gained nothing. Kevin was able to pressure the Pittsburg quarterback on a few pass-plays (although was not able to sack him that day). And San Ramon won that game, on Pittsburg's field, by the way. I came away from that game thinking: *Jeez, I knew he was strong. But I didn't know how strong was his **will.***

The debate on football continues in America. Maybe someday it will be outlawed. As for Kevin, I know he was injured a few times. But I know that allowing him to make his own decision and playing football was necessary to his empowerment and his exploration of his potential. He needed validation, as we all do. He needed an outlet for his drive and his underlying ferocity. Like all parents, I have some regrets. But allowing Kevin to play football was not one of them.

On the Fringe of Cool

If "Nerd-Introvert-Awkward" is on the left end of the spectrum, and "Cool-Charismatic-Successful" on the far right, I think Kevin lived just right of center. He was athletic and always had a group of casual friends. But he was also socially awkward at times, sometimes painfully so. Once in Natick, when Kevin was about seven years old, he asked a neighborhood friend, "Who's your best friend?" He did this within earshot of me and Marilene, so his friend, understandably feeling put on the spot, even at the age of seven himself, said, "I don't know. Don't ask me that!" The friend was of course justified, as Kevin's question was ill-timed and needy. Internally, I winced for Kevin. Was I really raising a kid this desperate for acceptance and validation?

A few years later, Kevin at the age of ten played little league baseball in Danville, California. After one game, I saw him chatting with one of his friends in the dugout. A minute later, as he walked over to me where I was waiting to take him home, I could see in his face that something wasn't right. So I asked him, "What's up?"

"I asked Jason if he wanted to come over. But he said our house is too boring." Kevin's upper lip was trembling. He was on the verge of tears.

But he didn't cry. He took a deep breath, somehow composed himself, and then said, "Oh, well. I guess I just need to find more friends." I processed a few different feelings. At first I felt a pang of sympathy for Kevin's apparent snub. But then the speed with which he composed himself and moved on almost startled me. Hell, when *I* was upset or aggrieved, I could stay that way for *hours*. How could a ten-year-old so quickly put such a snub behind him? He didn't get that from *me*.

Later on, in high school, Kevin wanted to be a part of the cool football crowd, but he always seemed to be on the periphery. He would join most of the parties, and he might occasionally hang out with some of the guys. But he didn't seem to be top of mind for them when the coolest guys hung out together. I don't know which hurt more: not being asked to hang out, or that knowing sense that you were not even in the consideration-set of people to hang out with. That familiar ache of wanting to belong came flooding back to me from my own teenage years: the awkward attempts to be cool and accepted by the chosen group; the inevitable face-plants; the girl for whom I pined, but who went with (and later married) one of the cool guys; my envy of the effortless ease and confidence and sharp humor of the cool crew. It was no different for Kevin. And it's no different for perhaps 95% of young people. Arguably, it's a rite of passage for almost all teenagers. Intellectually, of course I know all this. But it doesn't change that acute pain that I felt as a father of a young man desperate to belong, to be validated, to be included, but often to be disappointed. I think that pain as a father affected me more than my own as a teenager.

When Kevin was in a funk, I supported, encouraged, and sometimes commiserated with him. I complimented and emphasized his strong points to boost him. I shared stories from my own teenage years to show that the same things happened to me, that I understood. Kevin was usually stoic, not often expressive. In hindsight, I doubt that Kevin got any special revelations or nuggets of fresh wisdom from these chats. He was sixteen, or seventeen, and of course so worldly that he was way past being able to learn anything from a *parent,* gimme a break! But if there were no "aha's" in those chats, at least what passed between us was that I cared. And maybe that was what mattered, anyhow. Maybe that was enough.

Cancer

We need to talk about cancer. We need to talk about it not because of what it took away. We need to talk about it because of how it shaped Kevin, and us, and what it revealed.

It started in December 2014. After his sophomore football season was done, we noticed a knot at the back of Kevin's left thigh. We thought it was a muscle knot and would work itself out. When it didn't, Kevin tried to roll it out with one of those firm styrofoam cylindrical rollers you use at the gym. But it hurt him, so we took him to the clinic.

Now the tension climbed. Some imaging revealed a mass about 4 centimeters by 13 centimeters. The doctors ordered a biopsy at University of California San Francisco (UCSF). We took Kevin there. When I say "we" I mean Marilene and I both went with him for the biopsy appointment. Over the next three and a half years, we tried whenever humanly possible to both be there for appointments and consultations with doctors. We succeeded almost every time.

The biopsy doctor gave Kevin a local anesthetic on the back of his thigh and then pierced it from two different angles with biopsy needles to extract some of the mass. Those extracts would need to be sent to a lab for analysis. The procedure lasted all of maybe fifteen minutes. We would have to wait a day for the results to come back.

And so began a lengthy, rhythmic relationship with the health care system, over the next three and half years. The experience drew from the complete palette of the human and emotional spectrum. We found deeply caring and (here the Spanish word rings in my head) *simpatico* people, the kind of people that touch you deeply and not just transactionally. We remain in touch with some of these people even now, well after Kevin's death. It is because they are such caring people, and we know that Kevin feels good about us keeping those links. We also, to be fair, encountered more "transactional" people, and even a few times incompetent people. When this happened, we asked right away for hospital administration to replace them. We had no time for—nor wanted to subject Kevin to—the "training" or grooming of people into more seasoned doctors or nurses. Perhaps many of them will grow into caring, nurturing people over time. It is a journey for us all. We insisted on caring, competent nurses and doctors, and for the most part the folks at UCSF were exemplary.

The biopsy came back as a form of cancer called *rhabdomyosarcoma*. Cancer occurs in less than 3% of young people. But of those rare cases, sarcoma accounts for about 60% of them.

I went with Kevin to our first meeting with the oncologists at UCSF, after the rhabdomyosarcoma had been diagnosed. Understandably, Kevin and I were both tense. Think of the context and the stunned numbness. Kevin had started his sophomore year in high school just four months before. He had played two successful seasons of football, had a girlfriend, was part of a team and a group, and had started driving at his sixteenth birthday just five months before. In so many ways, he was living his dream. Cancer happened, but it happened to *other* people. Now, you're thrust into a meeting where your very future hangs out there with a "To Be Determined" sign hanging on it. It's like holding your breath, submerged in the deep end of the pool, legs and feet flailing, not knowing if you'll be able to push off the bottom, push up and explode through the surface to take a deep breath of air.

Kevin and I gathered in a smallish examination room. The UCSF team came in. The lead oncologist was an older woman, tall, rail-thin, wearing glasses, and with a teacherly way about her. We will call her Dr. McCord. Dr. McCord was accompanied by a younger doctor Dr. Wong, male, about thirty-five, as well as three other people.

After settling in, Dr. McCord jumped right in, directing her gaze and her comments to Kevin, with glances at me to test for comprehension and acknowledgment. "Look, I am so sorry you're having to go through this. We can't tell you the cause. And you shouldn't try to guess." She paused. "Look, we can fix this."

Kevin and I both exhaled. Dr. McCord continued.

"We have gone over all your tests, imaging and biopsies with our tumor board." We came to learn that these "tumor boards" are a common practice in cancer treatment. It's a panel of experts who discuss and agree on treatment protocols.

Dr. McCord went on to explain what they wanted to do. First, they would shrink the tumor with chemotherapy. Next, they would perform surgery to remove the shrunken tumor. After that, radiation to treat the area to ensure that any stray local cancer cells were killed. Finally, four more months of chemo to kill any cancer cells which may have traveled, but were not visible on any body scans.

Dr. McCord shared the side-effects of the various treatments. In almost all cases, patients went through fatigue, nausea, diarrhea, loss of appetite, and hair loss. Also, chemotherapy rendered almost 100% of patients sterile.

The whole plan would consume eleven months. Dr. McCord reassured us that most of their patients had been able to stay at the grade-level of their peers in school, and—with few exceptions—graduate with their class.

The room began to feel quite close. Kevin asked for air. I guessed that he was feeling faint and went out to find a chair he could rest on briefly in the hall. In those handful of seconds, his feet buckled under him and the team had to catch him and help him back to sit down. He went pale and looked shaky. After a few minutes and a cup of water, he recovered enough for us to finish the meeting.

So we left UCSF that day a bit numb from what we had heard. We were in for a challenging year. But we steeled ourselves. I put my arm over Kevin's shoulder as we descended to the parking lot.

"You're not in this alone, buddy. We're all with you on this." It felt feeble, clichéd. But I was too distraught and wound-up myself at the moment to come up with a more comforting way to say it.

Before we started the chemo protocol, which would sterilize him, we needed to take Kevin to the fertility clinic. This is common for anyone about to undergo chemo. The patient deposits a sperm sample. The clinic keeps and freezes the sample. Then, X years later, the cancer survivor (and partner) decide they want to have kids. Unfreeze the sample, perform an artificial insemination, start a family.

Okay, so business as usual for the fertility clinic, surely. But we're talking about a sixteen- year-old, accompanied by his *parents.* And he's facing sterilization. Had this been me, I would have been queasy, maybe nauseous, at the prospect.

But this wasn't me, it was Kevin. And what struck me about this episode—and several others, throughout our journey with cancer—was the "Let's get on with it" attitude Kevin showed. Upon pulling up outside the fertility clinic, he could have said, "Jeez, Mom and Dad, couldja wait in the car or go have a coffee or something?!" But all three of us went up to the second floor. We checked Kevin in. Soon, they directed him to a room, and—I suppose—a sterile jar and some magazines. Marilene and I sat in the waiting room for maybe fifteen minutes. Kevin returned, and we left. I remember thinking: *How could he be so unselfconscious about it all?* It struck me then, and still, that many forty-year-olds would be embarrassed and timid about the indignities thrust on you when you go through something like this. Where Kevin obtained his poise, his "I don't care; let's get on with it" persona, I can't say. Maybe from Mozart.

Chemotherapy turned out to be a mixed regimen of drugs. Some were given on an outpatient basis: we would take Kevin to John Muir Hospital in Walnut Creek for a two-hour infusion in the afternoon, after school, and then home. Other drugs required overnight stays in the hospital at UCSF Mission Bay in San Francisco.

All these drugs were tough, but one in particular, irinotecan, just ravaged Kevin. Irinotecan (ih - rin- oh - TEE – can) made him retch, gave him diarrhea, whacked his appetite, and rendered him basically horizontal for days. Sometimes, he convulsed with dry heaves at the same time he sat on the toilet with gut-cramps and diarrhea. One or the other of us would bring him a bucket for the vomit and a cool wet washcloth for his forehead. Kevin would groan for hours. Marilene, Gustavo, and I tried to help however we could, the whole house tense and wired, sometimes for days until the toxic worst passed. Sleep was patchy, nervous, shallow.

A few days after the infusions, once the worst effects had passed, Kevin mostly resumed himself. Many parents these days complain that their teenage kids play too many video games. But, I can tell you that after Kevin had been through a rough chemo session and the aftermath of the next few days, it was pure music to our ears when he had a few friends over, playing video games, laughing, shouting—hell, even cursing.

Kevin's high school, San Ramon Valley High, rallied around him right away. We came home from the hospital as it was getting dark to find two girls staging lanterns along either side of our driveway. A big group of kids had taken brown paper lunch bags, written encouraging and supportive notes on the sides, and cut patterns into them. Then they weighted the bags down in the driveway with a couple fistfuls of sand in each. Finally, they placed little electronic votive candles in the sand so that each bag was lit from within. Pulling up to the house, it was a warming sight. Kevin soaked up the well-wishes. He wasn't vocal or animated; he just seemed satisfied, content with the support and recognition.

A week or two later, the same student group had a bunch of yellow long-sleeved tee-shirts printed up. They said "Stronger Than Sarcoma" on the front and "Mad for Madsen" on the back. A group of fifteen or twenty of them wore the shirts at mid-court at halftime at the next varsity basketball game. We were unable to be there, but friends sent us pictures, which of course we shared with Kevin.

Once news of Kevin's diagnosis spread, the head coach of the San Ramon Valley High Football program offered to stop by the house. Kevin had played two years of football by this time. He would have played varsity in his junior year, but for the cancer. We hoped the coach could give him a pep talk.

The coach came by the house around 7:00 p.m. I couldn't have scripted it better. He said he was sorry Kevin had to go through this, but that he wanted Kevin and needed Kevin to come back to the field once he'd kicked this thing. The coach looked Kevin in the eye and spoke to him like a man. Kevin took it to heart.

About five weeks into chemo, we saw more and more hair on Kevin's pillow and in the shower drain. The odds had been low that he would escape this side-effect of the chemo, but we had held out hope. Kevin was upset, understandably enough. He knew that it was likely he'd lose his hair. But knowing it is one thing, and when confronted with actually losing it…well, he took it hard.

Knowing beforehand of the likelihood that this would happen, one or two of Kevin's closer friends had offered to shave their heads with him in solidarity. This idea took on a life of its own. Before you knew it, we had broadcast a Head Shave With Kevin Solidarity Day at the local Sportclips. A dozen of Kevin's friends showed, from football, rugby, soccer, and school.

At Sportclips, there were four chairs available at any one time, and a dozen or more guys getting shaved. So they had to go in shifts. Kevin was one of the first in a chair. I later learned of an odd coincidence: the lady shaving Kevin's head had lost a son to cancer some years back. I was taking pictures to commemorate the event. As the lady began to run the electric trimmer over his head, and swatches of hair tumbled down, revealing pale, bald scalp, I caught Kevin's eye in the reflection off of the mirror in front of the barber's chair. As he watched another patch of his hair hit the floor, his throat caught, his lip trembled. He was about to sob.

At that exact moment, a friend in a neighboring chair cracked a funny joke, which got Kevin and all around laughing. It lightened the moment immediately and clearly took Kevin out of himself and just at the right moment, too, for which I was immensely grateful.

I took a picture of the entire crew with shaved heads, a mountain of hair swept into a pile in front of them. Sportclips said it was on the house. We went next door for pizza at Garlex afterwards. I wanted to pay but Gary Martinez, the owner, wouldn't let me.

Kevin finished the day bald, but what his friends did for him that day meant a ton to him.

He would be bald for months. He even lost his eyebrows to the chemo, so he had a slightly alien look to him. But I noticed something one day when I picked him up from school. I halfway expected him to slouch, to shuffle, to try to be inconspicuous, as he crossed the quad at school to meet me. Instead, I saw a comfortable young man, striding with ease across the quad. He stood out, to be sure, because he was bald and fairly pale. But he pulled off the bald look better than most of us would, and he appeared to have no self-consciousness about him at all.

We got to the car, hopped in, and I drove off. Kevin shared an anecdote from school that day.

"Dad, I was cruising through the halls between classes. This kid comes up to me and says, 'Hey, what's up with the bald look?' So I said, 'It's *cancer,* man!'"

I was trying to gauge if Kevin was upset by this exchange. "So…how did you feel about this?"

"Well, after I told him it's cancer, I said, 'And I can *still* kick *your* ass!' The kid walked away."

"Hah!" I let fly. "Good for you, dude!"

Perseverance

Kevin was fifteen days into a 28-day radiation treatment regimen. This particular morning, our dear friend Ashly Kwon gave Kevin and Marilene a ride over to USCF in the morning. Leaving the house at 6:30 a.m. got them over to UCSF by 7:45. In the Radiology Department, Kevin walked to the back to the treatment room. He would recline with his leg in a mold of sorts, fitted exactly to him. This mold was designed to position him exactly the same way every time, so that when he was wheeled into the machine, the radiation beams would pass through him in exactly the same location every time.

This treatment was designed to kill stray cancer cells in the area where Kevin had had surgery, at the back of his left thigh. The side effects of radiation included nausea, localized burns on the skin in the area of treatment, hair loss (which did not affect Kevin, as the chemo had already taken his hair), and a cumulative, deepening fatigue, which grew as you went further into the treatment cycle.

The treatment itself did not last long. When Kevin went back to the treatment room, he returned no more than fifteen minutes later. They had another appointment in the East Bay. They headed off to Walnut Creek to John Muir Hospital, where Kevin would have a chemo infusion over ninety minutes or so.

Kevin dreaded chemo infusions but got on with it. On the trip over to Walnut Creek from UCSF, as Ashly drove, Marilene and Kevin squeezed some numbing gel from a tube and smeared it on the skin over Kevin's port. The port looked like a lump beneath the skin, about an inch and a quarter in diameter, sticking up about a quarter of an inch above the surrounding skin. The lump was caused by a surgically implanted plastic "junction," which in turn led to high-volume veins near the heart.

Nurse Nancy at John Muir—Kevin's favorite, and a dear, caring lady—was best at accessing the port in Kevin's chest cleanly and the first time. After cleaning and sterilizing the numbed skin, she first cleared and rinsed the port by injecting a few cc's of saline solution. Kevin, always sensitive to tastes, could often taste the saline in his mouth within seconds of her dosing the solution into the port. Unfortunately, that saline taste often made him nauseous, so we always had a pink bucket at the ready during these sessions, in case he had to upchuck, which was often. Over time, Nancy got to know Kevin well, and she learned how to perform the saline step with as little saline as possible, and Kevin got sick far less often. We dreaded the days that Nancy was off; Kevin had to admonish whoever the stand-in was to go easy on the saline.

During the infusion over almost two hours, Marilene continued to keep buckets at the ready. The drugs would usually make Kevin sick several times over the course of the infusion, even if Nancy administered anti-nausea drugs at the same time. Marilene would keep at least two buckets: one at all times by Kevin; the other to be dumped into the toilet in the restroom nearby, rinsed, and fresh paper towel lining the bottom, to suppress any splash-back.

On this particular day, the infusion wrapped up about noon. As they walked out to the car, with precautionary pink buckets, because the nausea persisted for some time after the infusions, Marilene asked Kevin "So, you want to go home, Kevin?"

"No," he answered. "I'm gonna keep my AP Euro Test."

He was speaking about the Advanced Placement Test for European History. Months before, I had reserved and paid for this AP Test for him. When you take college-level (that is, Advanced Placement) courses in high school, the way you receive college transfer credits for them is by taking the AP Test for that subject. In addition, the AP courses carry higher credits than the normal courses, so your grade is worth more in an AP course than it is for a normal one. Many of the best students pack their schedules with AP courses to make them more competitive in their college applications.

Of course, I had reserved and paid for this AP test well before we knew we would be in cancer treatments, well before we knew that Kevin would be in radiation treatments *and* chemo when this day came. If I had thought about the AP Test at all, it would have been simply to tell Kevin to forget about it. I had no expectation that he would go.

Marilene pressed Kevin. "Are you sure about this, Kevin? Neither Dad nor I would blame you if you just blew this test off. You've had radiation and chemo in one day. It would be totally understandable if you didn't go."

"No," Kevin insisted, "I'm gonna keep it."

"Can I at least get you something to eat before you go?" Marilene pleaded.

"Thanks, Mom. But I just can't." Kevin tried to let her down easy. He usually was unable to eat for several hours after one of these infusions. Marilene knew this but had to offer, at least.

And so, after waking at the crack of dawn, after a searing radiation treatment, after a ravaging chemo infusion, with the associated retching that went with it, having not eaten that day, Kevin was dropped off at the school for the AP Euro test that afternoon. It would last three hours.

And he passed that test, too.

Marathon

Kevin was sixteen when they diagnosed sarcoma. At UCSF this meant that he was treated in the pediatric oncology ward. At eighteen, you're treated as an adult in a different ward.

So Kevin was one of the oldest patients on the pediatric ward at any given time. When we were there for more than a day, we would try to get in a walk or two around the floor each day, just to get Kevin out of bed. Since he was hooked to an IV, we needed to drag a rolling metal tower with the liquid chemo bags and saline bags hung from hooks at the top, strung with driplines connected to a tube fed into a "port" installed surgically on Kevin's chest near his collarbone. The infusion port was an innovation in cancer treatment sometime during the prior ten or so years. Before ports, they used to infuse chemo directly into veins in the arms. The problem was that the drugs are so toxic they 'burned' the veins in the arms. Our own nephew Caio in Brazil had confronted testicular cancer just ten years before. Many times his nurses had been unable to find viable veins in his arms for an infusion, so they would stick and re-stick Caio, sometimes several re-sticks, causing Caio, about twenty at that time, to cry from so much pain. By inserting a small port under the skin near the heart, doctors could introduce the chemo into the body in a spot where the blood flow was more rapid, mitigating the burn issue, and disseminating the drug throughout the body more quickly and efficiently.

In some part of my brain, I suppose I thought that the port was a pretty slick and novel innovation. But that part was compartmentalized somewhere way off, away from what consumed and dominated most of my daily thoughts.

On the walks around the Pediatric Oncology floor at UCSF we saw many young kids. Some we saw walking with their exhausted families, dragging their own IV towers. Some were pushed in strollers with built-in IV towers, clutching stuffed animals or superhero dolls. Others we saw only as we passed their rooms when the door happened to be open. They were often asleep, mouths open, clear tubes in a nostril. Many were bald, like Kevin. Many had the pale, sickly look. Once I saw a baby less than a year old with a port surgically installed on its chest, for administering chemo. I had to look away and collect myself, hoping that Kevin hadn't seen the baby or my reaction.

Kevin and I had a lot of time to ourselves on these hospital stays. We tried to focus on future things. Sometimes we talked about him mentoring young children undergoing cancer treatment. Other times it was about returning to working out to get back into football shape. Yet other times we spoke about selecting colleges to which he would apply. In fact, we completed his St. Mary's College application during a five-night stay at UCSF.

School was tough, tougher than we had been led to believe. Within weeks of his first chemo treatments, it became clear that Kevin would not be able to stick with the full schedule he had started with that semester. Chemo itself often kept him from class. Then recovery from chemo often kept him out of even more classes. Especially after an irinotecan dose, Kevin was laid up for days afterwards.

So we dropped classes, changed others, and finally got Kevin some credits from independent study which allowed him to go on his own hours, when he was feeling up to it. Then in summer, we supplemented what he had done during the regular school year with paid tutors for math. Kevin desperately wanted to keep some classes at San Ramon High so he could see his friends. We supported that.

How painful, how cheated, must a teenage boy feel in Kevin's situation? These years are supposed to be your runway to your future. All you want is to belong. All you want is to chase girls, hang with the guys, play a sport if you're halfway athletic, get a car, start creating a little space for yourself, some independence from your parents, and set your sights on a decent college. So often, Kevin must have felt himself on an island, watching the party boat sail off. He was left scratching and clawing, trying to keep his dreams possible, at the same time scratching and clawing for his very life.

The treatment program went as planned. After eleven months of chemo-surgery-radiation-chemo, of retching and weight loss and diarrhea and hair loss, of missing most of his social life and girls, and after eleven months of jerry-rigged school schedules and desperate clawing from behind, the scans showed that Kevin was clear. It was fall 2015. Kevin had missed football his junior year, for obvious reasons.

Our good friends the Rivases and the Nelsons surprised us with a celebration for Kevin's milestone. They—along with several others from the community who helped—rented out a hall at the Danville Community Center, and they even hired a regionally famous Motown cover band, "Pride & Joy."

Almost two hundred people came. It was multi-generational. Many of Kevin's schoolmates came, of course. And many of their parents. A number of the coaches and some teachers came, as well. Great food, drink, music, dancing; this party had it all. Our friends Gil and Mike shared a few words. I made a speech about Kevin's journey and his recent clean scan, and I told him how proud of him I was, which got a number of people emotional. The climax of the night came a couple hours later. Kevin's brother Gustavo and a bunch of Kevin's friends spontaneously lifted Kevin up over their shoulders and passed him through the crowd, up in the air. No marathon winner ever grinned more.

Chemotherapy often changes one's hair, when the hair returns. It will often change both the color and the texture of the hair.

Kevin had always had straight blond hair. After he was through his chemo regimen in late 2015, a few weeks later Kev's hair came back on a *mission*. But in place of his straight blond hair, he now sported a wavy, tawny mane. It looked good bursting from his football helmet.

Comeback

Once he had been declared in remission in the fall of 2015, and the port in his chest was removed, Kevin started to work out right away. He had seven months before summer tryouts for football, in what would be his senior year at San Ramon Valley High. He attacked eating and working out with a vengeance. It was gratifying for us to see him so motivated, so driven.

He also had much life to catch up on. Most of 2015 had been wiped out by the ordeal with chemo-surgery-radiation-chemo, with the accompanying baldness and sickness from the poisonous treatments. Kevin wanted to resume a normal social life, which he felt he was owed.

And, he had to catch up academically, to stay on track for a decent college. So he stayed with a special schedule throughout his junior year, keeping two core classes at San Ramon High, so he could stay with his social circle. That was supplemented by the independent study program, which was based twenty minutes away in the city of San Ramon. By now, he could drive himself to that one.

The academic requirements also needed to be augmented with summer study in trigonometry. So in the summer of 2016, Kevin would go to football practice every Monday to Saturday from 8 a.m. to noon. He would come home and shower, grab a quick lunch, then he'd go off to his afternoon session with his trig tutor over in Walnut Creek. That summer was for Kevin much busier than almost any of his peers. He got after it with determination. His grades during the school year were B's and a few C's; understandable with all the treatments. But that summer, he aced trigonometry.

Varsity

It's October 2016. Kevin is pissed.

No one worked harder than he did, to get his weight up and get back into shape. Remember, most of the football players didn't lose much weight in their offseason. Kevin dropped thirty or forty pounds when on chemo. But he worked and ate like a demon. And he did it. He got back to 205 pounds and recovered all his quickness and power, even though the back of his left thigh was slightly thinner than his right, due to the muscle mass they had had to remove along with the tumor.

Throughout the summer workouts, Kevin felt he got the better of the peers competing with him. A number of his friends on the team agreed that he was stronger.

But the coaches were starting two guys ahead of Kevin. He didn't know why. He thought he was better than they were; he always beat them in practice. And damn it, he'd *earned* it!! Privately, I speculated that the coaches worried about starting a guy who had cancer last year. I could understand that, even if I thought it was woefully unfair to Kevin. If they only knew what it *meant* to Kevin, how hard he worked to get back here, how he had his eye on this horizon all through surgery and chemo and retching. And Kevin hadn't forgotten the chat he had had with the head coach, saying he wanted him back on the field; he *needed* him. You or I might muse that the coach was simply saying what he thought Kevin would want to hear. But Kevin never sparked to nuance or subtlety. He took that pep talk exactly at face value. He felt that the coach—the program—had reneged on their promise, and that they were starting inferior players.

The coaches had made clear since freshman year that they wouldn't discuss playing time with parents. They were trying to raise young men here. The players were expected to raise any concerns with the coaches, themselves, one-on-one. Kevin met with the coach making the line decisions and asked him, "What do I need to do to start?" Coach offered some vague generalities about being a little quicker off the line, but nothing which persuaded Kevin that he was not being treated unfairly.

We were about seven games into the San Ramon Valley Wolves varsity season, and Kevin fumed on the sideline. Just before gametime, suddenly one of the starters was hurt, so Kevin got sent in. He played that whole game at right tackle. He made almost all his blocks (he admitted he missed one), both on runs and passes, executed well on pulling plays, and the Wolves won the game. Afterward, Coach complimented him on the game. A week or two later, Coach saw him and admitted he should have started Kevin all season.

That measure of vindication did not assuage all the roiling Kevin did for three months at the first part of the season. It did not place him overnight where he felt he properly ranked among his peers. But it did in its way validate Kevin as a man. It did give credit for the hard, relentless work he had put in. It did say: You were right; I was wrong. So we closed the chapter on the fickle, unfair nature of high school football.

And we needed to, because we now had to turn to other things.

Round Two

The week following Kevin's solid performance in that football game, the school called. Kevin—looking pale and sweaty—had told a teacher he didn't feel well. As he said it, his eyes rolled up in his head and he passed out. The teacher caught him but needed help to gently lower him to the floor. The school called 911, then us. I sped over to the school and pulled up to see the ambulance in the quad, Kevin already in it. They told me they would take him to John Muir in Walnut Creek. I followed.

Kevin had bled internally. They gave him a transfusion and sent him home with an antibiotic because they thought he had a bacterial stomach infection and a bleeding ulcer. But he passed out again the next day. Back to John Muir, he was scanned and they found a mass at the tail of his pancreas, and up against the spleen. So the cancer was back. Kevin needed surgery fairly urgently, since internal bleeding was a big risk.

Since he had been treated for cancer at UCSF, John Muir felt that Kevin should return there for the surgery. They did not want to risk sending him all the way to UCSF in an ambulance at rush hour; it might take too much time and the bleeding could get bad quickly. So they opted to fly him over in a helicopter. Again I followed, on wheels.

At UCSF, they removed the tumor, along with a third of Kevin's pancreas and all of his spleen. Once he stabilized, it was time to meet—once again—with the oncology team.

The mass that had been removed was the same rhabdomyosarcoma Kevin had fought before. So clearly the thing was not killed, and equally clearly it had travelled from his leg up to his abdomen...and who knew where else?

Dr. McCord and the oncology team recommended a different chemotherapy regimen this time. The first cocktail hadn't worked, so we would try something else. When we were in a separate room from Kevin, I asked Dr. McCord what the chances of success were.

With a curl of resignation to her lip, she replied, "Well, less than fifty percent."

This felt like a kick to the solar plexus. I had to take a deep breath. Marilene began to cry, tried to compose herself.

The odds in the aggregate population, I later researched, were that only 17% of people who get it a second time are alive five years later.

So what do you do? You can give up. You can lament your rotten luck, second-guess everyone. But you owe your son your best possible you, no matter what.

And 17% DO get through it. And many of the 83% that don't are the very young, the very old, the otherwise infirm. Kevin was none of those. In fact, before all this Kevin was healthy and strong beyond belief. Whatever the odds in the aggregate population, the odds for the *individual* are either 100% or 0%. One out of six (~17%) make it, and I'd wager that my son was stronger than most of those folks. We had to think of it that way. We had no choice.

And so, Round Two began. Surgery done, Kevin embarked on a new chemotherapy and radiation protocol. You may ask: If the tumor was removed in surgery, why the radiation and chemo again? The answer is because the cancer cells can (and in Kevin's case clearly did) travel. Surgery treated the largest and most-problematic localized issue of the moment: the tumor causing internal bleeding. Radiation treated the local area, with the intent of mopping up trace or missed cancer cells. And chemo targeted cancer cells system-wide.

The only "good" thing about Round Two was that the hated irinotecan was not on the menu. So Kevin was less sick this time. But one drug needed to be given in a hospital stay over five days and nights. That drug had a cycle every three weeks, so one week in three we spent five days and nights together at UCSF. I had just left my job in a restructuring, so I suspended my efforts to seek a new one so I could stay at the hospital with Kevin each time. In addition to the five-day stints, Kevin received infusions of other drugs on an outpatient basis.

Some of the chemo drugs are so toxic that the nurse would dress up in a head-to-toe haz-mat suit, complete with gloves, slip-on booties, and a hood with a plexiglass face-shield. She (or he) then had to cross-verify the drug, dosage, and confirm the patient with a second nurse before hanging the bag and hooking it up to Kevin's dripline. A bag would typically drip (that is, infuse) over 90 minutes to two hours. Then they would follow the harsh drugs with saline drips over the next several hours. Kevin peed into plastic bottle urinals with measuring lines on the side. Nurses kept careful records on urine output. When he needed to poop, we had to unhook some of the pulse- and temperature-monitoring devices, hang the bags on the rolling metal tower, and drag the rolling tower into the bathroom.

Often several times a night, an alarm would chime, and a nurse would come into the room to turn off the alarm and to check if everything was okay. It turned out that Kevin's heart rate was tripping the alarm; it was too slow. His resting heart rate was like that of a marathoner, even though he was never a long-distance runner. His heart was unusually strong. The alarm would chime and wake us both up. So I asked the nurses to re-set the parameters on the heart monitor to lower numbers, explaining that Kev had always had a strong heart and a much slower than average heartbeat (even going back to the womb! Recalling the frantic nurse bursting into the delivery room just before he was born, because his heart rate alarmed her). But the lowest they could set the tripwire at the low-end of the range was 40 beats per minute. The problem was, Kevin regularly went to 37 or even 36 BPM in his sleep. So despite all the state of the art technology at UCSF, sometimes mundane, simple things frustrated us.

Scarcely two hours ever passed without a visitor. If it wasn't the nurse taking vitals or administering chemo, saline, or oral drugs, it was the nutritionist, the physical therapy technician, the community service provider, the chaplain or other spiritual counselor, the in-house teacher, the Oncology Department Nurse Practitioner, or the house-keeping crew.

And then there were of course the doctors. We had oncologists, pain doctors, surgeons, imaging doctors and technicians. They came in singles, doubles, triples, and—when the teaching docs were on "rounds"—they came with a dozen learning doctors in tow.

Visits from friends meant the world to Kevin during those long stretches at UCSF. But not all visits were created equal.

Friends

If you wish to weed your pool of friends, have a crisis. Whoever you think of as friends now, that group will change dramatically when you face hard times. That sounds like a threatening or negative thing. I don't think it is a negative, though. To be sure, it hurts when you face the disappointment of the disappearing friends. But you emerge from it in a better, stronger place, with friends who mean something to you, who you know will be friends the rest of your life.

In our family's case, the crisis was Kevin's cancer. But we all know people suffering from one or another crisis. Health issues, job losses, divorces, natural disasters.

We had a number of friends we thought were quite close. They vanished when Kevin got sick. Ours was not a huge community, so we would run into them from time to time at school events, the supermarket, or church. They would come up to us, go through the theatrics of concern—a hug, a hand on the shoulder or grasping the elbow as if to help out of a car, a "Call me if you need anything." They picked from the menu of acceptable gestures, offered up tokens of sympathy, then returned to their families, issues, careers, and lives, not to be seen nor heard from.

That sounds harsh, or like criticism, but isn't intended to be. I have come to believe that we all come to extend our love and support to others according to our abilities and capacities to do so, at the times and places which strike that one vibration on the tuning fork, the ones that pull you out of yourself, the ones that call you. I myself—in an earlier version of me, in this lifetime—was not equipped to lend emotional support to others in need. I was afraid: afraid of failure, missteps, inadequacy. I think many if not most people live in that space, and our society is the worse for it. People must grow through—or be shocked through—that stage, must answer the calling when it is presented. As someone once said: It is its own reward. How true that is, and how expanded is your quality of life when you open and offer of yourself. I hope that there's a new Renaissance soon: one of feeling, community, and true charity.

Another group of people we thought of as acquaintances, or as social but not intimate friends, turned out to be angels. They showed up unasked. They brought meals, care packages, cookies, brownies. Our good friend Marci Nelson outfitted a binder for us to organize all Kevin's appointments, tests, diagnoses, phone numbers, and medications. We had no idea how useful this was going to be; Marci researched it and just went out and did it for us. Ashly Kwon often drove Marilene and Kevin over to San Francisco; Marilene is a little intimidated by freeway and urban driving, so Ashly's help was a godsend. Laura Rorke did the same, and always made Kevin feel cared for and cared about.

A Tutorial on Visiting
People in the Hospital

I once feared visiting sick people in the hospital. I didn't know what to say. I didn't know how to "be" with them. I avoided it and felt guilty about avoiding it. I learned later that many people—maybe most people—felt as I had in the past.

An experience like ours jolts you to the other side of the fence, mighty quickly. I remember times when friends texted or called Kevin that they were coming to visit him at UCSF. You could see him animate right away with the anticipation. Remember, we had five-day stretches in that place; the hours yawned in front of us, promising only a shift-change for the nurses and a fresh bag of liquid on the pole to break up the monotony. Kevin so looked forward to just cutting up a bit with some of the homeboys. But a number of times, after friends said they were coming, the rides didn't come together, or something came up, or they just couldn't get around to it. Kevin's disappointment was palpable. He deflated, visibly, and his day—no picnic to begin with—was unsalvageable. Marilene and I got so angry with his friends sometimes, which of course we never shared with them. The friends hadn't *intentionally* inflicted pain on Kevin. But nonetheless they had hurt him badly. They couldn't see what we did, or they would never have treated it so lightly.

When you have a friend in the hospital, please don't fear visiting them. And when you visit them, please don't walk on eggshells worrying about what to say. Just be yourself, chat normally with your sick friend. Trust me, your sick friend craves a little normalcy right now, and you can serve up a little. And it will mean so much to them, you simply cannot imagine. If your sick friend is too sick to engage in conversation, just sit with them, read to them. Let them know you're pulling for them. Your visit will take a few hours of your time, but the gift you give your friend might recharge them for a day or more. If you give a little support or encouragement to a sick friend in a moment of despair, you might actually save a life.

Trading Places

On our long stays at UCSF, I slept in Kevin's room. The rooms had couches that converted to beds. One night after Kevin was situated, I did up the couch with all the bed linens, drew down the shade on the window, doubled the pillow, and climbed into bed. I lay awake for a few minutes, and I knew that Kevin was still awake.

"Kev, I'd give anything for this to be happening to me instead of you, buddy."

A few seconds of silence passed before he spoke. "I know you would, Dad. Thanks."

"I love you, son."

"Love you too, Dad."

Marilene

Marilene always kept a positive, brave face on in Kevin's presence. She fussed over him, prodding him to eat, or to have a shower or bath, or just to brush his teeth. Kevin adored his mother, loved her visits to the hospital, but he could get irritated at the fussing. Sometimes he snapped at her. She did an admirable job letting it roll off of her when he did that, most of the time. Anyone in Kevin's situation could get thin-skinned; I was amazed he kept it together as well as he did, frankly. I think I would have been insufferable.

But beneath the brave face, Marilene was frazzled. She slept little, often taking hours to fall asleep, and then sleeping only three hours. She ate irregularly, and—privately—cried often. We tried to buck each other up. We also wanted to be there to support Gustavo, as much as possible.

Among her support group, Marilene counted on several of our close female friends from Danville, as well as on her sister Maristela who lives in the Bay Area. And, when they could come visit us from Brazil, she got immense support from her sisters Marcia and Mariza. During their visits, more Portuguese was spoken in the house than English, and we all inhaled the aroma of our next home-cooked Brazilian meal. Marilene soaked up her sisters' love and support like a sunflower, and his aunts' presence and loving care buoyed up Kevin during times when the waves were crashing into his little boat. Gustavo and I also loved having Marcia and Mariza, and Chloe did, too! She often slept with one or the other of the sisters, preferring their company over ours!

When she could get them, walks helped Marilene cleanse and recharge her energy. If one of her good friends was available—like Marci Nelson or Ashly Kwon or Laura Rorke—she could have a cathartic chat along the trail. They often hiked six or more miles. And hearing about others' kids and families took her out of herself for a much-needed break.

Another thing Marilene absolutely loved was cooking for Kevin's (*and* Gus's) friends when they came over. She had always hoped and wanted that ours would be one of the boys' preferred hang-out homes. And the boys all loved her cooking and seemed comfortable at our house. They were welcome to stay quite late at our place, playing video games or watching some movie. When they left, Kevin always felt he had had a good day. We went to sleep gratified.

But whatever forms of support or distraction relieved her temporarily, what awaited her every night—what stared back at her from our bedroom ceiling for hours on end—was that hated but inescapable question: What Could I Have Done Differently?

Hollywood

On the five-day stints at UCSF, when I stayed with Kevin, Marilene would come and stay for a few hours, which would give me time to get a shower or to go outside, take a walk or go to a nearby restaurant. The hospital food got old in a hurry.

In good weather, I would walk down a mile or so to AT&T Park (now Oracle Park), where the San Francisco Giants play. Returning, I would keep to the sidewalks and trails closest to the bay. It made for a scenic walk and some decent exercise.

One day, toward the end of my walk, I was passing by the bay near the drydocks just east of UCSF. I took casual notice of a guy fishing from the rocks to my left, at the same time playing a radio with a game on. About fifty yards further up, I noticed another fisherman.

As I passed adjacent to the first guy, he spoke.

"Man, what about that Pete Carroll up in Seattle, eh? What the fuck is he up to?" For readers that don't know, Pete Carroll is the coach of the Seattle Seahawks of the National Football League.

It wasn't at first clear if this was for me or was rhetorical. I looked over.

"Oh, man. Don't *even* get me started!" I affirmed. I paused my walk. Pete Carroll has always gotten under my skin. My new acquaintance and I bantered a few minutes about the Seahawks latest trade maneuvers, then on to the latest woes of our own Forty Niners.

"How they hittin'?" I asked, motioning at his fishing pole, which he had jammed into the rocks, awaiting a jerk on the line.

"Dinner's in that bucket." He nodded over at a large white painter's bucket, covered with a piece of cardboard. I walked over to him as he lifted the cardboard. A couple of decent-sized smelt flapped in some water. "Yeah, those will do you up, proper." I acknowledged. "How you cook 'em?"

My acquaintance was an African-American guy, about my height but with broader shoulders. He wore a beret, a Forty Niners jacket, and creased jeans.

"Here's whatcha do," he answered. "Ya fillet 'em, salt and pepper, a little garlic, some lemon, a little olive oil, and grill 'em up five minutes on a side." He formed the thumb and fingertips of his right hand into a point, brought them to his lips, and smacked them. "Perfect!"

I laughed. "Sounds good. Sounds like you've had some practice."

"Oh, yeah. Since I moved outta the house, I'm down here most every day in good weather."

It turned out that Darryl, as I found out was his name, was fed up with his wife because she had allowed her daughter and son-in-law to move into their place, against Darryl's wishes. The son-in-law, to hear Darryl tell it, was a deadbeat, had even taken one of their garage parking spaces, fer Chrissakes. So Darryl got himself an apartment and said he could not stomach the coddling of the son-in-law. And here he was.

Just then I heard the theme music from *Jaws*, the part where the shark is circling. Puzzled, I looked around. "What's that?" I asked.

Darryl fished his phone out of his pocket. "That's her," he said. He hit the button to silence the chime; didn't answer the call. "That's my wife. I don't need whatever she's sellin' right now. She's gonna say, 'You want some tonight?' an' I'm gonna say, 'That deadbeat sumbitch still there?' and she's gonna say, 'Aww, come on, baby, don' be like that. I got the *itch*. Don' ya wanna scratch it?' an' I'm gonna say, 'Scratch that yo' *own* damn self!'"

This was getting too good to rush back to UCSF.

I learned that Darryl was a retired builder. One claim to fame was that he had worked on John Madden's house in the East Bay. I say "claim" because I have no way to verify that, but as Darryl might have said, "It didn't make no nevah-mind to me, anyhow!"

I glanced over at Darryl's fishing companion, fifty yards up the shore. He was an older Asian man, butt on rock, elbows on knees, fishing pole waiting.

"Who's got the better spot?" I asked Darryl. "Him, or you?"

"He ain't catchin' nuthin'," Darryl said, looking over that way with a sly grin on his face.

To my surprise, the old Asian man must have heard Darryl. "Fuck you, Horrywood!" he said, loud enough to reach us.

Darryl grinned and chuckled.

"What did he call you?" I asked.

"Hollywood. That's my nickname. That's about all the English he's learned, Chinese son of a bitch." He grinned over at the old Asian.

Again, "Fuck you, Horrywood!" These two clearly had an understanding.

Darryl—or Hollywood, as he now unavoidably came to be known—and I chatted on for another twenty minutes. He asked me what I was doing here. I explained about Kevin, getting treatment up there (I pointed at the sixth floor of UCSF). Hollywood got serious.

"Hey, you keep the faith now." he said. "That's the best place in the world for this kinda treatment. They got good people there. I'll pray for you and your son. You bettah get back on up there. Your wife's waitin' on ya."

"I appreciate that, Hollywood." I thanked him. "I get this way pretty regularly. I'll look you up."

"You do that, bruthah. Like I said, I'm here most days in good weather."

I finished my walk back to UCSF and took the elevator up to the sixth floor. Walking back into Kev's room, I shared with him and Marilene the entertaining little diversion from my walk.

Over the next couple months, I saw Hollywood two or three more times on my walks. Sometimes I saw him solo; other times I ended up chatting with him and two or three other people who had stopped to chat with him, and were also on a first-name (nickname) basis. Hollywood was well-known, and a magnet in these here parts.

A couple months later, Kevin needed labs drawn (read: blood test) in the morning at UCSF, followed by a gap in the day before an early afternoon appointment. I took Kevin for lunch over at Mission Rock Resort, a favorite seafood spot of mine a couple blocks from UCSF, overlooking the bay. Kevin and I scored a table on the deck, next to the railing—sailboats, gulls, and buoys just below. The table was shaded by a large deck umbrella. The sun shone, and the deck was warm.

I suppose these moments with Kevin, just him and me, over a nice meal in a terrific setting, are among my fondest memories. Certainly it was a father-son moment. But for me, it ran deeper. One of us was a man by virtue of age and a measure of what the world calls accomplishment, most of that accomplishment behind him. The other was a man—at the age of eighteen—by virtue of test, trial, and grit. The scales of raw character tilted decisively in Kevin's favor. He was more than a man through my eyes; I wonder if I ever made him understand that.

We enjoyed a wonderful lunch on the deck. Afterward, we still had some time to kill before the afternoon appointment.

"Let's go see if Hollywood is fishin' today," I said. Kevin, remembering my stories, was immediately game. Hollywood's favorite fishing spot was only two hundred yards from Mission Rock, so we did not have far to walk. Sure enough, he was there.

"Hollywood!" I greeted him, as we walked up to his spot.

"Hey, bruthah!" he replied. He likely met so many people that names may not stick. But it was clear that faces did.

"Wantcha to meet my son Kevin." I motioned to Kev.

As the two of them gave each other a hearty handshake, Hollywood remembered. "You're the one gettin' treated here, yeah?" Kevin nodded. Hollywood had started to release the handshake, but now, he held it a few seconds longer as he spoke, directly to Kevin now, and he placed his left hand on Kevin's right shoulder.

"You listen, partner," he started, his eyes on Kevin's. "You keep on with the keepin' on here, you hear me?! You can kick this thing, goddamn it. You strong, you got good people helpin' ya. I'm prayin' for ya, man, ever since yo' dad told me aboutcha."

Kevin was moved, and pleased that this stranger showed up so strongly in his corner. But he already had some window into Hollywood's personality from my earlier stories.

We chatted with Hollywood another twenty minutes or so. Both he and Kevin had played high school football, so they could share war stories. Hollywood offered sage advice: "Don't do no drugs, now. You can smoke some weed, but don't do no pills and don't *ever* inject nuthin'!" Later, Hollywood somehow shared a story about some cops who had tried to ticket him for parking his van near his fishing spot. The encounter had grown tense, and soon one cop turned into three.

"An' I said, 'This is bullshit!'" Hollywood said, as he re-enacted the scene. "So I squared up in front of one of 'em, and I said, 'Fuck you!' Then I turned to the next one, and I said, 'An' fuck *you*!!' And then I turned and faced the third one, and I said, 'An fuck *YOU*!!'" Somehow Hollywood emerged from this anecdote without going to jail or getting injured. Must be a charmed life.

Finally, Kevin and I needed to leave to make our afternoon appointment. We said warm goodbyes to Hollywood, said we'd see him again. As we walked, Kevin said, "Man, I gotta bring my *friends* over here to meet *him*!"

Angels come in many—sometimes unexpected—forms, on many different missions.

Unfinished Business

Kevin and I had an errand somewhere in the North Bay area. On the drive home, we fell into a silence. Something had been on my mind, so I asked Kevin about it.

As background, the something to which I refer is rooted in an argument we had at the family dinner table when Kevin was thirteen. I can't even remember the run-up to the heated moment, but at its climax Kevin was hot.

"I guess we can see who's your favorite son!" he spat, directed at me and Marilene, implying that we favored Gustavo over him.

I don't even remember what discussion triggered Kevin's vindictive attack. But whatever it was, it hadn't prevented that episode from gnawing at me for six years. So in the car that afternoon coming back from American Canyon, I brought it up.

"Hey Kev, there's something that happened a long time ago, but it's bothered me ever since. There was this time over dinner. You felt unfairly treated for some reason. What caused it I don't actually remember. But what you said was 'I guess we know who's your favorite son!', implying that we preferred Gus over you." I paused. "Did you ever really feel that, son? Do you feel that way now?"

A few seconds passed, while Kevin was silent. I was driving, so I had my eyes on the road. Suddenly, I realized that Kevin had his hand to his eyes, squeezing them against tears. A sob escaped him. A second or two later, he lost the battle against the tears, and just let them come.

I was taken aback. I had hit a sore spot, obviously. Keeping my left hand on the wheel, I reached over to him and rubbed his shoulder and then rubbed the back of his neck as he had his head in his hands. I tried to comfort him, glancing back and forth from him to the highway.

"It's okay, son. Sorry if I hit a nerve. I didn't mean to upset you."

A few minutes later, we pulled into the driveway at home. As we walked up to the front door, Kevin stopped me. He was crying again, but he managed to get out between sobs: "Dad, after what you've done for me the last two years, believe me, I know you guys care." We hugged. We held each other tightly, for quite a while. He sobbed several more times before halfway regaining himself. We walked up the path with arms over each other's shoulders, to the front door.

Maui 2

In summer 2017, after Kevin graduated from high school and before he started college at St. Mary's, Marilene had an idea.

"Why don't you take Kevin to Hawaii, just the two of you? Have some quality father-son time."

This was after Round 2 of cancer treatments. Kevin felt well. We both liked the idea. Kevin remembered fondly our family trip to Maui five years before. He wanted to go back there. So we made plans.

Our flight got us to Maui early in the morning. But our check-in time at the Hyatt at Ka'anapali wasn't until 4:00 P.M. We killed the time with a helicopter tour which looped the entire island, seeing things one can only see from the air, because parts of the jungle are so dense that neither horses nor vehicles can get in.

Kevin and I passed a wonderful four days in Maui. But no trip there is complete without a visit to Mama's Fish House. Kevin flagged that weeks before we even went, so I had secured reservations while we were still in California. We went to Mama's on Day 3.

Kevin would never have described himself as sentimental. But every once in a while, he'd maybe leave a window open into how he truly felt. Call it sentimental. Call it family nostalgia. He had a special place in his heart for Mama's.

What can I say about being a father, and letting your son know that he's worth it? That the trip clear across the island for forty minutes there and forty minutes back is not a problem? Not only is it not a problem, but you look forward to a drive with your son, you look forward to that one-on-one time, uninterrupted by someone's cell phone, unbroken by a text from someone, the reggae music seducing you into island-time. That two hundred dollars is nothing, compared with the quality of the time you are spending together? That what he has done is far bigger an accomplishment than not only what you have ever *achieved*, but far bigger than what you have ever *attempted*? That he has earned your respect, beyond what he can ever possibly know? That no father was ever prouder of his son.

Mama's did not disappoint. We had another magazine-review-worthy dinner, the two of us. We talked of his freshman college-year about to start. We talked of career aspirations. Of travel. We talked about a future that you would wonder if you could cram into one lifetime.

A few weeks later, back in California, I needed to use Kevin's truck for some errand. I borrowed his keys, said I'd be back in an hour or so. Hopping up into the truck and starting it, my first order of business was to tune in some music. I raised my hand to the buttons, then stopped. There, on the little display which showed Kevin's music choices, was a complete reggae playlist.

St. Mary's

Kevin started his freshman year of college at St. Mary's with far more ease and confidence than I would have expected. St. Mary's is a small school, so perhaps not as intimidating as a major college campus. In any case, on his regular visits home from school—we lived just thirty minutes away—Kevin shared that he liked his classes and the school in general. He wasn't thrilled with his roommate, but then that happens to many in their freshman year. He worked it out.

Within a few weeks, Kevin said that he had clicked with a small group of friends. Marilene and I were surprised but pleased. We hadn't thought of Kevin as extroverted enough to have so easily and quickly cottoned on to a crew. And this crew had both guys and girls, so we felt good about how he socialized from the get-go.

As parents, we took a deep satisfaction from Kevin's regular visits home. I imagined that many freshmen might revel in the freedom from home and parents and would seldom visit them even if they lived close by. But Kevin seemed to get something soothing or reinforcing from visits home, even if they were only brief, thirty-minute visits. On one such visit home, Kevin shared an interesting anecdote from school.

"I was just standing in the dining hall in a crowd after eating," he began. "Then some guy taps me on the elbow. I turn to face him. He asks me, 'Hey, are you that Madsen kid, from San Ramon Valley High? The one that beat cancer...twice?' So I stand there for a second, wondering, *Where is this going?* but I go ahead and answer him 'Yeah, that's me.' Then the kid says, 'You're a hero, man.'"

Kevin recounted this little story matter-of-factly, his eyes focused at a distance, no particular pride in it. To him, it seemed an odd little novelty, a rare peek into how others saw him and his story.

"And you are that," I offered back, gratified that my own view of him was shared and validated by someone in the crowd.

Dylan

It was September 2017, Dylan hunched at his keyboard in his dorm room at St. Mary's. His roommate was out, so he had the place to himself, which he preferred when he was composing music.

A knock at the door. *Dang!* Dylan thought. *Who's that? And just when I'm on a roll.* He crossed over to get the door.

Kevin was there. "Mind if I hang?" he asks.

"S-S-Sure," Dylan replied and waved Kevin in. They had gotten to know each other some, but were not bosom buddies—at least not yet, in Dylan's view. "But I'm writing some music. If you don't mind just hangin' while I write, that's cool."

"Solid," Kevin acknowledged. He strode over to one of the bunks and reclined there, perusing something on his phone. Dylan returned to composing.

An odd—and to Dylan, surprising—comfort with all of this soaked into the room. He continued composing for another hour, he and Kevin exchanging not so much as a word, with no awkward silence vibe whatsoever. Had you told Dylan before this that it could be this way, he'd have looked at you sideways.

When Dylan achieved a measure of satisfaction with the song he had composed, he and Kevin agreed to go out to Kevin's truck, play it on his truck speakers, and to smoke some. They played and replayed the song. Kevin offered a few suggestions, which also surprised Dylan, and some of the suggestions actually resonated. They stayed in the truck for an hour, playing a number of different songs, and talking.

This became a ritual with Kevin and Dylan. Kevin would drop in, as he knew when Dylan—and Dylan's roommate—had classes and when they didn't. Dylan welcomed Kevin with a "Hey." They settled into their roles with the ease of the familiar. They would camp out there in Dylan's room, sometimes for a couple hours, in each other's worlds yet each in their own, too, completely relaxed, accepted, and understood: Dylan in the creative, meditative state; Kevin somehow able to be there in silent, patient support, saying nothing, and without sending ripples into Dylan's zone. Afterwards, the pilgrimage to Kevin's truck, the music, a little smoke, the chats that solved the world's problems.

Here, Dylan describes it best:

As time went on and we got to know each other more and more, Kev also started to gain an understanding of how I should express my music. At first it was just a silent connection where we were just appreciating each other's company and we bonded over the talks and the time in the truck. But after a while he started to help me on specific tracks and actually help me write some stuff. He became part of the process. Instead of sitting silently on the bunk, he would sit next to me and I would run pretty much every sound by him. On one hand it was great to get a second opinion, but on the other it was to get an opinion that I knew held importance.

The ritual changed a little and the talks became deeper. He started to pick up different technical words and we were able to talk about songs in what was beyond simple layman's terms.

It was a sign that I knew this was something which held great importance for him, which also made it quite important for me. While this wasn't even half of the things we did together, it was something which I felt we bonded over in an incredible way. It was something which was super personal for me but Kev turned it into something which was personal for the both of us. To this day I have yet to find a "non-musician" (a word I hesitate to use) who has such an interest into the personal side of composing. I think it speaks to Kev's personality and the bond which we had together.

The acceptance that Kev gave me with my music is something that is so powerful it's hard to put into words. A lot of time people will give my song a quick listen and a "That sounds great!" but Kev went beyond that and I could physically tell he wanted to play my songs in the truck ALL THE TIME, not just because they were my songs but because we could understand each other through what we had made. Partly because he might have been there when it was produced, but also because he had an otherworldly desire (which I still don't fully understand) to respect/ promote/acknowledge the creativity behind the work. Kev is someone who truly saw the things I found passionate [sic] and made it something that he was passionate about as well. That is a skill that I have yet to find anywhere else, even within myself.

Later, Kevin and Dylan invited Claire and Hannah into the space they had created. It was a magical, perfect blend: two males, two females; the creation and enjoyment of Dylan's music, the others chiming in ideas; the warm blanket of acceptance and genuine affection; the place where you simply show up as you, because you know the others bring that and they want that of you, as well as they would sniff it out and tell you if you started to veer into bullshit, because that was the license you had given them, that was the quality you *wanted,* you *needed,* from them. And they loved each other, and each felt better about themselves for it.

When asked how the group formed, they all said the same thing: it had formed around Kevin. With him, they each found something new in themselves, some unknown quality or talent, or some untapped potential.

Kevin and Claire shared the same English professor, Professor Cooney. After one of their assigned essays, Professor Cooney had each student come to one-on-one office hours to go over their papers.

As Kevin departed Cooney's office, Claire waited in the hall for her appointment. Cooney's parting words as Kevin opened the office door were: "And you got the best grade in the class."

Kevin met Claire's gaze briefly as he stepped out of the office. As Claire stepped forward, passing Kevin to keep her appointment with Cooney, she elbowed Kevin in the ribs and muttered under her breath, "Bitch!"

Love Jones

Kevin was smitten.

Three weeks into his freshman first semester at St. Mary's College, Kevin stopped by the house. He lived on campus in a dorm, but our house was only 30 minutes away, so he swung by frequently.

On this visit, Marilene was at home; I was still at work. Kevin wanted to chat with her, anyhow.

"Mom, I met this girl." Kevin started. As much as the words, the anticipation in Kevin's voice brought Marilene to full and undistracted attention.

"She's independent. She does what the guys do. She's real confident. She's bright, too." Then, the ultimate compliment: "You'd really like her."

In the following weeks, we heard more about Claire, Kevin's crush. They were already fast friends. Claire was part of the small group of new friends Kev had formed. To hear about her, we pictured a tall, lean girl, with long, dark brown hair with curls, intelligent, tomboyish, and she glided through the halls at St. Mary's as if she were a senior with all her graduating credits safely in the bag. In fact, she was a freshman, just like Kevin.

But of course, Kevin wanted them to be more than good friends. Just one problem: Claire had a boyfriend. Kevin met the boyfriend some weeks later. He told Marilene he was a very nice guy.

So Kevin bottled his feelings and poker-faced it. The circle of friends socialized together often. Kevin loved their company, all of them. They got quite close; did everything as a group. They were loyal and caring with each other.

But Claire's face was the last one on his mind before he fell asleep each night.

Round 3

I took Kevin to UCSF for his regular CT-scan one day in October 2018. We were a bit tense, since this would be his first scan since the end of treatment from Round 2. But Kevin looked and felt fine. Two months into his freshman year at St. Mary's College, he seemed to be enjoying it, and had started a few new friendships there.

CT-scans usually consumed a morning over in San Francisco. Kevin and I crossed the Bay Bridge over into the City along with the rest of the morning commute traffic. We were veterans of these scans by now. Kevin must have had eight of them by then. On other trips into the City, he often reclined his seat and slept. This time, he didn't seem sleepy. We chatted—about school, politics, our upcoming trip to Brazil over the holidays. We chatted about everything but the obvious.

We did the scan routine within about ninety minutes, and were on our way back to the East Bay. We would hear about the scan results the next day.

The next day, Dr. McCord called my cell. After an exchange of pleasantries, she got right to the point.

"Listen, we see a new mass on the scan. It's just behind the bladder, and it's about the size of a lemon. I am so sorry to have to share this news."

Ohhhhhh, No, No, No , No, Noooooooo...!!!! Hasn't he been through ENOUGH !!!??? WhyWhyWhyWhyWhyWhyWhyWhyyyyyyy? God, this isn't FAIR !!!!! These thoughts overloaded my mind, but for the moment I didn't speak.

You thought you'd awakened from your nightmare, only to discover that you'd awakened into *another* nightmare. Twice, now.

My mind and heart were imploding. Marilene, standing nearby and seeing my face, knew right away. She began crying and ran outside to the front lawn, fell to her knees, hunched over, and slammed her fists into the ground, cursing in Portuguese.

All of this took seconds. Dr. McCord was patient. With effort, I summoned up a question from whatever sector of my mind still functioned.

"Okay, that is disappointing news," I started, feebly. After a pause, "What treatment options are available now?"

"Well, we've tried the traditional or textbook treatment options, and obviously they haven't worked. So now we're on to the world of clinical trials."

I was scarcely able to follow much, after that, through the numbness I felt. But I did retain that a different doctor at UCSF handled the clinical trials. So we would be put in touch with him, a Dr. Sallis.

I hung up after thanking Dr. McCord. I went to try to console Marilene, or to have her console me, I don't know which. Through her tears, she managed to get out a few words, between sobs.

"It's not fair!" she forced out. "He's so happy at school now. How are we going to tell him this?"

In that moment, I had no answer.

Kevin came home from St. Mary's that afternoon. He was in a bouncy mood. This was two months into his freshman year at St. Mary's. He had started reasonably well in his classes, was building confidence academically. Plus, he had already begun to forge a small network of new friends, which probably pleased him even more than the academic side. We chatted about how he was doing for several minutes. But the agony of what we had to share with him next hung there, like a lead weight, sitting in our guts.

Kevin made motions as if to leave, to return to school. I was just about to detain him, tell him the awful news. Marilene pre-empted me.

"Listen," she said to Kevin, "Dr. McCord called earlier. I'm sorry, Kevin, but they found another mass in your scan."

Kevin absorbed this, hung his head. The pained squint. The lips curling. The choked sob. Then, the tears came freely. Marilene and I went to him, locking him in a three-way hug, his head buried in my shoulder, sobbing now. After a minute or two of hugging, he broke the hug, and—still crying—walked over to the refrigerator and slammed his forehead into the top of it, denting the door to the freezer. It also opened a small cut at the top of his forehead, near the hairline.

Oh, what a miserable thing to have to do, to tell your son a thing like that.

Through all our dread and despair, we told Kevin not to give in, that we were by his side, that we would explore the clinical trials treatments with the new doctor at UCSF. We told him all the things you need to say as a parent in that rotten situation.

After that wrenching, emotional half an hour, Kevin said that he wanted to return to his dorm at St. Mary's. I asked him if he thought that was a good idea, if he was okay to drive. Marilene and I preferred that he stay with us. But Kevin said no, he was okay to drive, and he wanted to go back. We didn't have it in us to try to persuade him otherwise. The bouncing, upbeat young man who had arrived thirty minutes before left, replaced by a dejected, persecuted shell. We walked him out to his truck, wearing the bravest faces we could, kissed him and waved as he pulled out of the driveway, his face a gray mold. When he was out of sight, and we no longer had to act for his benefit, Marilene and I collapsed into each other's arms, buckled, distraught, agonizing at the universe, unable to comprehend. We walked back to the house, went into the bedroom, collapsed onto the bed, and held each other, crying until the tears no longer came.

Writing this now feels like the same punch to the gut as it did then. The only difference now is, I know the outcome. So the gut-punch isn't tinged with the last shreds of desperate hope. It's just about suffering, his and ours, and futility.

For the first time, we were forced to reckon with the prospect that we might not win this one.

Clinical Trials

The world of clinical trials felt like a desperate, confusing roulette. One number of that wheel might save your life; the rest yield death. The people who participate in these trials have already been through at least one—if not two—rounds of "traditional" cancer treatments. So for all practical purposes, this is their last hope.

After Kevin's third sarcoma diagnosis at UCSF, we sought second opinions and other, alternative clinical trials than were offered at UCSF. So we visited M.D. Anderson in Houston, considered by many to be the premier cancer treatment hospital in the country. We also visited a sarcoma-only specialist and clinic in Santa Monica. These people are some of the best in this field. In each case, we had them speak with Dr. Sallis at UCSF. After these discussions, the doctors all agreed that neither M.D. Anderson nor Santa Monica could offer a therapy better than what was on offer at UCSF.

So back in the Bay Area, we were faced with all the different lanes available to us, with their different starting points, side-effects, efficacy percents, and opportunity costs. And the experts could not coach us on which was the best path or option. There are simply too many variables, with too many trials, at different dosage rates, and with new trials opening all the time, for anyone to look you in the eye and say "Here's what I recommend." We were in uncharted territory, with an array of mediocre options, none of which popped as the clearly preferable one. And we were pressed.

The tumor had grown from nothing at the end of his treatments in Round 2, to the size of a lemon just ninety days later. So this was a fast-growing tumor. Some of the trials for which he would have checked all the boxes as far as eligibility would not start for 60 or more days out. We didn't feel we could wait that long to treat the tumor, so we opted for a more traditional oral chemo drug which had shown some success in arresting tumor growth (but not shrinking or killing it), frankly just to buy time. This drug was likely to take his hair—for the third time!—but it was not as debilitating on the nausea side. Therefore, it had the added benefit of allowing Kevin to make the December Brazil trip we had planned six months before.

So we embarked on Round 3.

Words & Music

Despite the new round of treatments, Kevin was determined to stay on track with his classes at St. Mary's. He was coming to love St. Mary's, his tight group of friends, and of course, there was Claire. Claire still had a boyfriend, but she and Hannah hung out with Kevin and Dylan constantly, and at such a small campus, the group became inseparable.

Kevin had created a playlist on the Spotify music app; he called it "Love." I had been aware of the playlist. I thought of it as one of Kevin's mood music playlists. But fast-forward twelve months. Gustavo and I were looking at Kevin's playlists, including "Love," when Gustavo jolted me: "You know that was to Claire, right? You know he loved Claire?"

Yes, I knew Kevin loved Claire. But as Gustavo and I recapped the songs on that playlist, I got goosebumps. Among the songs on Kevin's "Love" playlist:

☆ *Scar Tissue*	*by*	*The Red Hot Chili Peppers*
☆ *Could You Be Loved*	*by*	*Bob Marley and the Wailers*
☆ *Pretty Lady*	*by*	*Rebelution*
☆ *The Less I Know the Better*	*by*	*Tame Impala*
☆ *Forever Young*	*by*	*Alphaville*
☆ *Fast Car*	*by*	*Tracy Chapman*
☆ *Lean On Me*	*by*	*Bill Withers*
☆ *Brown Eyed Girl*	*by*	*Van Morrison*
☆ *Africa*	*by*	*Toto*
☆ *Your Love*	*by*	*The Outfield*
☆ *Ain't No Mountain High Enough*	*by*	*Marvin Gaye and Tammi Terrell*
☆ *Mrs. Robinson*	*by*	*Simon & Garfunkel*
☆ *Redbone*	*by*	*Childish Gambino*

But how could I have missed this? Gustavo was inescapably correct: Kevin had built this playlist completely around his feelings for Claire, and around the situation in which they found themselves.

Along with the goosebumps, I suddenly "saw" a vivid scene. It's nighttime. The four close friends—as they often did—sitting in Kevin's truck, talking, smoking, listening to music. Kevin sits in the driver's seat, as always. Dylan sits beside him. The girls occupy the back seat, Hannah on the left, Claire on the right. After playing some of Dylan's music, Kevin changes over to his "Love" playlist. As the songs play, the group grows quiet. Gradually, it becomes clear to everyone in that truck what is going on. Kevin's pain plays out in "Scar Tissue" and "The Less I Know the Better." To express his deep love for Claire he chose "Brown Eyed Girl" and "Africa" *("..take a lot to drag me away from you..... nothing that a hundred men ... could ever do...")* and "Ain't No Mountain High Enough." He pledges his everlasting friendship and trust with "Lean on Me." And for his most vulnerable, most desperate hopes for the future, he plays "Fast Car" and "Forever Young". It couldn't be clearer if Kevin had gotten down on his knees. Song after song, Kevin saying with music what he cannot with words, because Claire is spoken for. Kevin—Mister

Calm and Controlled as he cruised the halls and coolly greeted friends on the way—suddenly laid bare and completely exposed, to the girl and the friends he most cared about.

During "Lean on Me," Kevin lifts his eyes to his rear view mirror, locking eyes there with Claire. She returns his gaze for a few seconds, in silent, tortured acknowledgment of what he is doing, what he is saying. Her eyes glisten. She looks down into her lap and squeezes them shut for a moment, before looking out the window at the trees in the night.

Ben

The Grubaugh family lives in the Woodranch neighborhood, just a couple blocks from the house we lived in between 2006 and 2016. One son—Ben—was in Gustavo's year in high school, so one year behind Kevin.

One summer—it must have been 2014 or 2015—our house got toilet-papered. So we had the hassle of hosing all that mess down and off the trees. Then it happened again a few weeks later. We got wind through the neighborhood gossip grapevine that Ben was the culprit. When Kevin heard this, he was pissed. He stomped around the house and made noises about how he was going to resolve this, in no uncertain terms. This was during Kevin's football years, and he was in fearsome shape. I was also pissed, and part of me was right there with Kevin. But I talked him out of any confrontation with Ben; at least, I think I did. I think I would have heard about it if anything like that had happened.

Despite this episode of adolescent near-head-butting, Kevin and Ben became fast friends over the next couple of years. They would hang out regularly, and Ben became a steadfast friend for Kevin as Kevin suffered through cancer treatments. Someone at the high school had produced Beat Sarcoma rubber wristbands. Ben wore one for four years.

When Ben turned eighteen, being a young man of legal age, he wanted to get a tattoo. His parents (and our neighborhood friends) Kent and Kim did not get to weigh in on this. This was something Ben wanted to do, and to own. He researched it and went and did it solo.

On January 25, 2018, while they were hanging out in Kev's truck, Ben told Kevin that he thought he was the bravest guy he knew. He wanted to honor him somehow, and he thought that the tattoo was a good way to do it. He showed Kevin his new tattoo. It was a pair of Chinese characters on Ben's left side, over his lower rib cage. Ben explained that the sound of these two characters in spoken Mandarin is the closest approximation to "Kevin" that he could find: "Kai-Won." In Mandarin, Kai-Won means courageous and brave.

Kevin was completely unprepared for this unexpected tribute. His usual easy composure quavered. It cracked open a fissure within him, and from somewhere deep, where he shoved down and held all the pain and fear, it welled up until he could no longer hold it. It spilled over and through him. He squeezed his eyes vise-tight and pinched the bridge of his nose with his thumb and forefinger against the tears, but they would not be held back. Finally, the pent-up sobs erupted from his core, in wave after wave, and he became a passenger in the body he no longer controlled, his body gasping for breath between each heaving sob.

Urine Bags

In January of 2018, Kevin's belly began to swell, and his navel popped out some. In February, he began to have real challenges both urinating and moving his bowels. His lower legs began to swell. We took him to UCSF. There, the doctors informed us that Kevin's kidneys were shutting down. His body was starting to retain fluid. Soon his thighs also swelled.

A doctor visited us. It appeared that the tumor was encroaching on the urethra, preventing Kevin from eliminating urine. They could try to insert a catheter up through the penis to open the urethra and allow urine to flow. Or, they could surgically insert tubes into Kevin's back, directly into his kidneys. These tubes would extend out from his back about 24 inches and drain directly into plastic bags which would be velcro-strapped and hung, one at each thigh. This option is known as a nephrostomy.

The doctor described the options matter-of-factly. Kevin at that moment was lying face-down on the hospital bed, facing away from the doctor. When she described the nephrostomy approach, I could see his face; she could not. He looked up at me, his face twisted, distraught, protesting in silent anguish. Just the description of the nephrostomy distressed him so much that I had to wave off the doctor for the moment.

By the next day, the doctors reassessed the first—the catheter—option, and they realized that it might not work, if the tumor prevented its proper insertion. By this time, Kevin's legs had swelled to twice their previous size. Something had to be done, and soon. We finally agreed to the nephrostomy. When I asked how long the nephrostomy would be needed, the doctors gave noncommittal answers. I now realize that the doctors viewed the nephrostomy tubes as permanent.

They performed the surgery that same day; as these things go, this is considered a fairly minor surgery. Kevin returned to his room with the tubes stitched into and emerging from his lower back, slightly to the sides, and connected to clear plastic bags. The tubes and bags did the trick. Urine began to drain off immediately; understandable, since Kevin's body was carrying a significant excess. For a while, each of the two bags collected half a liter of urine every hour or two. These we unclipped from the tubes, then poured the contents into plastic urinals with measuring lines on the sides so the nurses could measure and record output. As the pressure in Kevin's body eased somewhat, the rate of drain slowed some. Over the course of three days, Kevin must have drained off more than 15 liters of urine. That's over *thirty pounds* of liquid weight. Gradually, the swelling in his legs went down. Through all this, Kevin was immensely uncomfortable, but as the fluid drained off and the swelling eased, he became more himself, or as much himself as any of us could be with tubes stitched into our backs draining off urine.

For the constipation, the doctors recommended Miralax, to soften Kevin's stools and permit them to pass. They had seen this situation before and felt confident that the Miralax would work. So Kevin drank Miralax mixed in water twice a day.

Early during this hospital stay, Dr. Sallis paid us a visit. At one point, he asked Marilene and me to leave the room. Kevin was nineteen, and certain things had to be discussed with him as an adult. We learned later that Dr. Sallis had shared with Kevin that there were no guarantees with any of the clinical trial therapies that we were working with. He asked Kevin if he (Kevin) had given any thought to how he wanted his quality of life to be managed. Kevin wasn't ready to have that discussion just then. He and Dr. Sallis agreed to table it for the moment, with a commitment that we would return to it soon.

When Marilene and I returned and Dr. Sallis had left, Kevin was upset. Dr. Sallis had made it sound as if Kevin's chances were much lower than Kevin had thought. Kevin thought we had somehow concealed something from him.

"Why didn't you guys *tell* me?" he implored. "I'll do anything. I'll even do the irinotecan again, if it will help." (Irinotecan was the most toxic of the chemo drugs that they gave Kevin in Round 1. It triggered terrible nausea, diarrhea, and vomiting, and basically eliminated Kevin's appetite.)

Marilene and I felt terrible that Kevin thought we had somehow sugarcoated the information. In fact, I think he had heard what he had wanted to hear sometimes. Dr. Sallis had said from the start of our journey into clinical trials that none of the drugs being trialed had more than a 20% chance of success, and Kevin had been with us when he said that. But if Kevin had engaged in "selective hearing," I later thought, I wonder how many of us would have done much differently, were we in his shoes?

Dr. Sallis was trying to get Kevin to think about and commit to paper an Advance Directive. An Advance Directive specifies what measures the hospital is authorized to take to save or sustain life and comfort, and also what measures they are expressly *not* to take. It was a reasonable thing to ask, under the circumstances. In fact, it is the doctor's obligation to seek the A-D when a patient becomes at risk of being incapacitated and unable to verbally express their wishes. We learned some weeks later that some at UCSF had wondered if Kevin would go home from the kidney shutdown scare. Since Kevin was no longer a minor, the doctor had to—by law—discuss this with him. But the whole episode jolted Kevin and us, and we were all pretty jolted and frazzled already.

But Kevin *did* go home from UCSF, nephrostomy bags in tow, velcroed to his thighs underneath baggy sweatpants.

More Important Things to Do

In early May 2018, as the Chief Financial Officer at the company, I sat in a meeting at work with maybe twenty-five people, including our CEO and everyone on the executive team. Someone in the meeting was talking about discontinuing some of the products we sold, as they were losing money. It was a worthwhile topic, one which deserved the full engagement of the CFO. But all I could think of was Kevin. Discussing discontinuing products just seemed trivial and irrelevant, compared to what I had going on at home.

I received a call on my cell during the meeting, so I stepped outside the meeting room to take it. Kevin was going to need a minor surgery. As I had for all his other surgeries, I wanted to be there for this one. I would have to take a couple days from work.

Then it hit me: I was doing justice neither to my job nor to my family. With Kevin, we were entering a phase when he would need a lot of support, regardless of the outcome. I wanted to be there, plus I could not leave all of that with Marilene; it just wasn't fair. So at the morning break in the meeting, I pulled my boss the CEO aside, informed him Kevin was to have another surgery, then further informed him of my decision to leave the company. I agreed to do three weeks of transition work before I left.

My boss was supportive, understanding. He even gave me a hug. I left the meeting soon after that. From the car, I called Marilene and explained that I had given notice of my resignation. She knew where my head was trending, but she didn't know that I would quit that day. In truth, I hadn't known it either when I left for work that morning.

A couple days before my last day at the job, the guy in charge of the manufacturing operations—we called him AJ—asked if he could buy me lunch. I said sure, but privately I was a little surprised. AJ and I had been in a number of meetings together, but we were not especially close. At work, he was highly regarded: a driving, hard-charging, no-nonsense kind of guy.

After a nice lunch, at which I actually got to know AJ a bit better, we returned to the office in his car. As we neared the turnoff, AJ said, "Hey, for what it's worth, I just wanted to tell you that I think you're doing the right thing, and I admire you for it."

I told him I appreciated his comment. AJ went on to say that, if he had become sick the way that Kevin was, he was certain that his father would not have made the decision I had. It seemed that AJ's father was highly career-driven. It was a wistful, poignant window into AJ's family and upbringing, and a slice of feeling from a guy who usually wore a steely shell.

It is interesting to hear others' feedback when they learn of my decision to quit work. Some thought it was impulsive, foolhardy, a risk to my career. Others applauded it, calling it brave. It was neither. I simply had a moment of clarity, where I realized that I served no one if I continued to try to work. At that point, it would have been dishonest to stay.

Relief lifted me right away. In hindsight, I realized that the building tension I had been feeling the last several weeks was tension at the prospect of *staying* in my job, not what most would expect: the stress of thinking about leaving it. I never for a second looked in my rear-view mirror. My only regret was that maybe I should have taken that decision some weeks earlier.

Maui 3

After Rounds 1 and 2 of Kevin's treatments, we explored not only the world of clinical trials. We began to explore, in parallel, some non-traditional approaches to healing.

One of our non-traditional experts was Dr. Warren Cranch. Dr. Warren, as we called him, was a certified chiropractor, but after he had suffered a near-death experience some years back, fighting Lyme disease, he discovered that he had new talents. He could feel and sense things he had never noticed before. So he began to study, to meditate, and to develop his newly discovered abilities.

We had been connected with Dr. Warren by another new friend, Kathryn de Silva. Kathryn, too, had been helping us with the non-traditional side of Kevin's treatment.

Dr. Warren lives in Hawaii, on the Big Island, but he makes regular visits to see clients in California. We saw him five or six times, even all together as a family sometimes. And we also did phone sessions with him. In the live or phone sessions, Dr. Warren usually took Kevin through some meditations, some of which drew out significant episodes from Kevin's life, which he still carried. An example of this was his grandfather Mozart's death, the day before Kevin's tenth birthday. Kevin, who would usually have no use for these "spiritual" dealings, liked Dr. Warren and went along with the sessions.

Once I had given notice in early May that I was leaving my CFO job by May 25, we recognized an opportunity to get over to the Big Island to see Dr. Warren the week after I wrapped up my job, and before we had to do the house move that we had planned for June 1. We booked it.

By May, Kevin was taking oral chemo drugs, and these took his hair away, once again. He had lost thirty or more pounds and appeared gaunt and pale. Worse than all of that, though, his belly was distended, like you see sometimes in photos of starving children, and his navel was popped out a full inch or more, like the end of a roll of quarters. He wore loose-fitting clothes, both to hide somewhat his pregnant-looking belly, as well as to accommodate the urine-collecting bags connected to his nephrostomy tubes.

We flew into Hilo, the wet side of the Big Island of Hawaii, rented a car, and established ourselves in a hotel not far from the airport. Dr. Warren, who lived about twelve miles away, visited us at the hotel three times over the following days. We spent two-hour sessions with him, diving deeper into Kevin's psyche. In between sessions, Kevin and I took walks around the surrounding areas. The hotel sat on Banyan Drive, and a few dozen banyan trees surrounded the area, their broad canopies shading the paths, their alien-like roots splaying out across the moist earth. At the water's edge near the hotel, we walked around several coves where families swam and played, and where large sea turtles fed. A park and a Japanese garden nearby also offered pleasing paths and trails, and we took advantage of those, too.

On three consecutive evenings, Kevin and I chose nice local restaurants for dinner. Kevin looked old enough that waiters and bartenders seldom carded him. If they did, he had a fake ID which always passed the sniff test. I hadn't known about the fake ID until just a month or two before this. When I did find out about it, it didn't seem like a battle worth fighting. At any rate, we had father-son cocktail hours each night, followed by some wonderful dinners.

After a handful of sessions with Dr. Warren, Kevin seemed somewhat soothed. We had to get back to California for Gustavo's high school graduation and our house move, so we thanked Dr. Warren, bid him goodbye, and planned to see him in a few weeks on his next visit to California.

Our return flight to the mainland was not a direct one back to Oakland. It took us first from Hilo over to Kahului in Maui. From there, we would fly back to Oakland. But we had a six-hour layover in the meantime. As we contemplated the prospect of that long layover, Kevin and I seemed to arrive at the same place simultaneously.

"Mama's?" we said at each other, in mirror image.

I rented a car, and we set off south from the airport. We had no reservation, but I was banking on the fact that we would arrive as they opened at 11 a.m., and we would find a way in. I dialed up the reggae music on the radio for the fifteen-minute trip.

Sure enough, at the reception desk at Mama's we were told that they were booked up. But, we could sit at the bar and order food there if we liked. "Even better!" I said. So, by 11:02 a.m., Kevin and I were seated at one of the bars just off the main dining room, chatting with the bartenders, their first customers of the day.

We ordered a couple of cocktails. Yes, it was 11 a.m. But we were at Mama's. We were going to enjoy this. We had a wonderful lunch, of two kinds of the freshest local fish, as usual.

I handed Kevin my phone and asked him to take a selfie of the two of us. He held my phone up with his left hand, the lens pointed back at us, and snapped.

I looked again at that photo a few weeks later. There we are at the bar, Kevin in the foreground, me beside and just slightly behind him, with my left arm draped over my son's left shoulder. Our drinks sit on the bar in front of us. At photo-left, sitting at the end of the bar, sits a lamp whose base is a woman in a grass hula-skirt. In the image, a tall plant stands behind me. To the right of that tall plant, and behind Kevin in the photo, is an arched stone wall. Within that arch, a wall of polished wood paneling, trimmed in white near the stone arch, holds a tropical painting mounted in a frame with white mounting board. The white mounting board behind him almost perfectly frames Kevin's face. In addition, the wood paneling behind him is so polished that it reflects the outside light coming into the restaurant, from where it opens onto the beach maybe thirty feet away from us.

Kevin and I are both beaming. He has no hair, but his dark-brown eyebrows are intact, and he has a light mustache and a full, close-cut beard going. You can tell from his face that he is not well, but in this moment, with my arm over his shoulder, his mai tai nearby, his grin as wide as can be, he is *happy.* And as you look more closely, you realize that—with the stone arch, the polished wood paneling behind him, and the white mounting from the painting framing his beaming face—Kevin is surrounded by light.

Early June

We needed to get back from Hawaii for a few reasons. Gustavo was graduating from high school. Their cousin Caio traveled up from Brazil, both for Gus's graduation as well as to see Kevin. And, we had a house move coming.

Gustavo graduated exactly one year after his brother. He strode down that ramp in his green cap and gown, diploma in hand, electric smile lighting his face. After the pictures with his girlfriend and all his buddies, he took one with Kevin.

I wince when I compare the photo from Kevin's 2017 graduation with the one from Gus's in 2018. In 2017, Kevin's color and weight appear robust, and the triumphant energy ripples off of him in waves. You can tell that there's substance under the shoulders of his green gown. He knows he's headed for St. Mary's College. He's looking forward to the beach trip to Southern California that most of the graduating seniors join.

In 2018, it's Gus wearing the green cap and gown. The young man beside him is recognizable as Kevin, in the eyes and the smile. He is smiling broadly, clearly proud of his little brother. But pale, hollow cheeks frame that smile, the eyes are slightly sunken. He wears a baseball cap backwards, to protect his bald head from the sun. His loose clothes hang from bony shoulders, the same shoulders which once filled—even stretched—his sweatshirts. And you can see beneath his shirt that his belly is distended, and I know that beneath his sweatpants are the nephrostomy bags, collecting urine because he cannot consistently pee anymore.

After Gus's graduation, we faced a house move. That is all a blur to me these many months later. We had downsized, so this would not have been as challenging a move as some of our earlier ones. But with Kevin's illness, it appeared a bit overwhelming.

But help swooped in in the form of Marilene's sisters Marcia and Mariza. They flew in from Brazil in mid-May, to stay for a month, to help us with Kevin as well as with the move. The house we were renting was too small to put them up properly. We had converted the garage into a man-cave (really a boy-cave) of sorts, so we outfitted that with a couple of makeshift beds. Marcia and Mariza never once complained. I think they felt that it was a little like camping.

I cannot overstate what her sisters' stays meant to Marilene, or to Kevin. Marcia and Mariza are two of my six sisters-in-law. But I think of them as sisters, and I greet them that way (in Portuguese) when we get together. In fact, the two sisters had visited us two other times during Kevin's long cancer journey. I call them "visits," but they worked throughout. They helped us move. They packed. They cleaned. They painted. They decorated. They cooked. They even massaged Kevin's shoulders and feet when he was in pain. Their stays included little to nothing of relaxing or tourism.

We also had help from Greg and Maristela, who drove over from Newark, about an hour away, on consecutive days to help out with the house move. With the many hands, the short distance from Danville to Walnut Creek—about seven miles—along with the fact that we had downsized by about half, we knocked out the move in a couple days.

June 24

Kevin retained so much fluid now that his scrotum and foreskin (he was not circumcised) ballooned up. "I can't even see my own penis," he lamented, tearing up.

Marilene helped him to the bathroom and stayed with him to help. Kevin was on pain meds, but not so much that they made him incoherent. He was still aware of what was going on.

"I don't want to die," Kevin implored, through tears, with his mom. "I want to be here with you guys."

Marilene, fighting back tears of her own now, tried to comfort her suffering son. She rubbed the back of his neck, cupped his face in her left hand, and stared into his eyes, about to speak. Kevin spoke first.

"Why didn't you guys *tell* me?" he asked, eyes red and brimming, in such a pitiful voice that all she could do now was cradle his head in her arms, stroke the back of his head, as her own tears now came freely.

Her voice breaking, all she could manage was, "You'll be okay, Kevin. You'll be okay," over and over. She began to doubt whether we were doing the right thing, constantly telling Kevin that he would find a way to fight through, that he was strong, that if *anyone* could beat this, it was him. But were we really doing the right thing? Were we avoiding the inevitable? Were we failing at this chance to say the final goodbye?

Guilt waited at the other side of either answer to that question. If we more candidly discussed the possibility of dying, would we simply trigger a self-fulfilling prophecy, and would Kevin give up? And if we *didn't* discuss death, would we cheat him of somehow better preparing himself, saying proper goodbyes to everyone he cared about?

Through our eyes in June 2018, I answer that question one way. Through our eyes of 2019, I answer another way. The "right" answer depends on what you bring to the party.

On June 24, it was an unanswerable question for us, or the time for when it might have mattered had passed. All that remained was to hug him close.

June 25

Despite all the fluid retention, Kevin felt well enough in the evening to go out with Gus and two of his best friends, Zach Iler and Grant Pisenti. Marilene and I were happy about this. He had had a tough week or so, and seeing his friends made him feel better than any medicine available.

The crew of friends had no special or scheduled plans; this would be just a hang-out kind of evening. They all piled into Zach's car, smoked some pot, talked, listened to music. They talked about their freshman years at their various colleges (except Gus, who had just graduated from high school). They talked about girls, cars, what they missed about high school and Danville. They talked about frustrations, and about hopes. They provided benchmarks for each other, and enough "dudes" and trash-talk that they all knew they belonged. After a while, they went to the Danville Foster's Freeze for some burgers, fries, and ice cream.

In the moment, it was similar to many other evenings the boys had hung out together. Only later, in hindsight, did they appreciate it for life.

June 27

The new house in Walnut Creek had all the bedrooms upstairs. Kevin was weakened enough by early June—and he had the uncomfortable bloat in his belly—that he avoided stairs whenever possible. He never actually slept in the room intended for him upstairs. He stayed on the sofa in the family room, just off the kitchen. And he never slept the night through, either, needing to get up a handful of times each night to use the bathroom, or to deal with pain. By the first week in June, Marilene and I had staged a mattress there on the family room floor near Kevin, where we both slept, so that one or the other of us could get up to help him to the bathroom at night when he needed it.

Kevin slept fitfully. I don't think he had a quality night's sleep in May or June. Sometimes, in his patchy sleep, he dreamed. On several occasions in June, he spoke Portuguese out loud, in his sleep. We could only catch words, not many sentences.

June 27. Marilene's sisters Marcia and Mariza were still staying with us, and Maristela was visiting that afternoon to help out wherever she could. At about 4:00 p.m., Kevin suddenly stood from the sofa with urgency. I thought he wanted to stretch his muscles, as he had done so many times the last few months. But he said "Ajuda!"--the Portuguese word for "Help!" Then his eyes rolled up in his head and he collapsed.

We caught him, or he would have fallen. The next thirty minutes were a blur. The frantic call to 911. Me desperately pumping my palms down hard on Kevin's chest. The arrival of the ambulance team. The transport to Kaiser Emergency. The helpless looks on my sister-in-law's faces, weeping as they looked on as I accompanied the ambulance.

At the Kaiser ER, only 20 or 25 minutes in a doctor came to me and said "Kevin has a low fever, which indicates an infection, and internal bleeding. Given his history, I have to tell you that we may not be able to do much for him. Does he have an Advance Directive?"

Now, I am sure that this doctor was doing his job, the best he knew how. But it felt somewhat clipped, cold and insensitive to me in the moment. I didn't like it. I steeled.

"To answer your question, yes, he has an Advance Directive," I began. Then I looked him right in the eye and said, "But you're getting way out ahead of us. We're not there yet. We're not ready." This guy obviously didn't know who he was dealing with. Even then, I held out some hope that Kevin could bounce from this.

They stabilized Kevin enough to move him from the ER to the Intensive Care Unit upstairs. Word seemed to have gotten around to our community. Over the next few hours people kept arriving to support and comfort us. The crowd reached a peak at around 11 p.m., when we had about twenty people crowding the halls and completely filling a small waiting room adjacent to the ICU.

Over the few hours between 8 p.m. and 11 p.m., friends and family came through Kevin's room, individually and in small groups, to murmur comfort and encouragement to Kevin as he lay unresponsive, the breathing tube down his throat, the rhythmic *Haaaa—Shhhhh* reminding you that he could not breathe on his own. Kevin was pale, bald, gaunt.

The ICU doctors advised us that Kevin had some form of infection and internal bleeding, confirming what we had been told in the ER. Now, in addition, organs were starting to fail. I asked if he would at some point be able to breathe on his own, and they were certain and clear: No, if the breathing tube were removed, he would stop breathing in short order. The decision no parent wants to make confronted us. To her credit, Marilene got there even before I did.

"We can't prolong this," she said. Her voice was clear and resolved, even as tears streamed down her face, which she dabbed almost constantly with a tissue. "His Advance Directive is clear in these circumstances."

It may only have been in that moment that I let go of my desperate hopes that Kevin might yet find a way to turn the corner on this thing, to produce that miracle that doctors would marvel at in conferences worldwide for years to come. We had passed three and a half years *knowing, believing* that our son was stronger than the doctors' consensus, that statistics meant nothing, that nothing could defeat that fierce drive in our warrior son. But now it dawned on me that my own fierce belief and desire for Kevin might be—in some sense—unfair to him. Was I keeping him here, in pain, past his time? Was I asking more, still, out of a simply exhausted fighter?

My dearest wife was not only strong, she was right. We huddled with Gustavo and told him where we felt we had to go. Gustavo questioned it for a few moments, but when he heard the details on Kevin's physical condition, and he was reminded of Kevin's Advance Directive, he agreed that we had to pull the breathing tube.

I went out to the ICU Waiting Room where most of our supporters waited, and also asked for those out in the hall to huddle in closer, and then I addressed our friends.

"Folks, we and Kevin appreciate so much all your support, how many of you came tonight. It means more to us than you can possibly know." I paused. "But it's getting on toward midnight, and I know that many of you have school or work tomorrow. I think it's time for me, Marilene, and Gustavo to be alone with Kevin. So again, thank you. We'll see you soon."

One by one, the friends and families began to trickle out. We had to deal with a few lingering goodbyes when we were in no mood to do so. But finally, the last of them departed the ICU.

Marilene, Gustavo, and I gathered around Kevin's bed, the hiss and shush of the breathing machine the only sound in the room. It was time to say goodbye.

Taking turns, we each went to the side of his bed, held Kevin's hand, and spoke to him. We told him he had fought beyond valiantly, but that he had earned the right to rest. We told him that he was loved here, and always would be, but that many who loved him just as much waited for him. We told him that we were proud of him and proud to be his family.

Finally, we advised the hospital staff that they could remove the breathing machine. The lights were lowered, the nurse and one doctor were very quiet and respectful. When they removed the breathing tube, Kevin's body took a few reflexive breaths—but not in a spasmodic way—before gradually relaxing. They recorded his heart stopping at 11:58 p.m., June 27, 2018.

Rest easy now, Lion Heart.

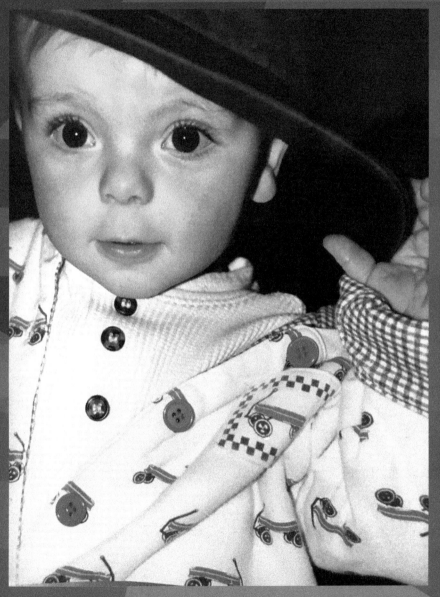

Kevin—One year old, in Chile in 1999.

Chile 2000. Kevin playing with an ice cube,
which for some reason makes Gustavo laugh uncontrollably.

Brazil beach trip—2007. Kevin nine, Gustavo almost eight.

Kevin in flight: a recurring theme, and the way I still always think of him. The above photo was taken in Sausalito, CA, in 2011 when Kevin was 12.

Kevin in three-point stance at football practice for San Ramon Valley High. Kevin played like he had something to prove.

Lion in tuxedo. After his first chemo, Kevin's hair came back as if it had unfinished business: thick, curly, tawny. This photo was blown up to placard size and placed on a stand at the memorial service.

High School Graduation—San Ramon Valley High, June 2017.
Graduating with a 3.1 GPA after two rounds of cancer treatment. Well
done, son!

Mama's Fish House, Paia, Maui. May 31, 2018.
I got to go to a bar with my son. Light all around him.

Photo of the seaweed-and-rose lei that Kev's good friend Hannah made in Hawaii.
She placed this on the beach at the water's edge the day of Kev's service.
Notice the "Kev" written in the sand in the center of the heart.

The red-orange dragonfly perched on Marilene's car's antenna, six days after Kevin passed.
This guy perched on her antenna for ten minutes, then took off, circled our house, and returned,
perching again in the exact same spot, facing in the exact same direction. It did that six times.
Some Asian and Native American cultures believe that dragonflies signify Transformation.

PART TWO

Donations

June 28, morning. Just the day after Kevin passed, my cell phone kept ringing. At first I simply declined the calls; I was in no mood to chat with anyone. But I noticed one number in particular kept ringing. When I saw that number once more on the screen of my smartphone, I finally answered.

After the caller introduced themselves and were kind to offer their condolences on Kevin's passing, it turned out that they had a good reason for their persistence. It was a society which harvests the corneas from people recently passed for transplanting to people with damaged corneas. Even now, some ten months after he passed, I wince at that word, "harvest." Maybe a better word is "salvage." In any case, they kept calling because they had a finite number of hours after he passed to be able to recover usable corneas, and of course they could not do so without our permission. I did a courtesy check with Marilene, but we both agreed Kevin would have wanted it, so we agreed.

Some weeks later we received a letter from the society, thanking us for Kevin's donation. His corneas were transplanted into two different people, one a 57-year old man, giving them both eyesight. This news was more soothing to me and Marilene than I would have expected. In a dark cave, I suppose any wisps of light magnify in importance.

Memorial Service

Eulogy, July 3, 2018
Given by Tom Madsen

Note: I have lightly edited the eulogy.

Thank you, Father Bob. For those of you who don't know me, my name is Tom Madsen, and I am Kevin's father. On behalf of myself, my wife Marilene, and Kevin's brother Gustavo, I want to thank you all for being here today to remember the life of an amazing young man. Some people have come here today from as far away as Brazil. I know of at least one person here from Alaska.

Kevin is half Brazilian, half Danish, and all warrior. Viking tradition holds that all true warriors pass on to Valhalla, and raise their mugs, toasting each other with the famous Viking toast "Skol." That image always makes me smile.

You know I have this immense photo album in my mind, with images of Kevin and our family. If you'll indulge me for a minute, I'd like to flip through that album for a few highlights.

I remember Kevin less than thirty minutes old, with his hand curled around my thumb.

I remember when Gustavo was born, and Kevin was first introduced to his newborn baby brother, and how carefully and tenderly Kevin touched his brother's cheek.

I remember Kevin at four or five years old, grooming his grandmother Lourdes's hair, there in Brazil.

I remember him nailing me in the face with a snowball, when we lived in Boston, and laughing out of his mind.

I remember him—the first time we went skiing in New Hampshire—and he pointed his skis straight downhill without any fear of falling or hitting anything.

I remember Kevin and Gustavo jumping off the artificial waterfall into our swimming pool—naked, of course—at our house in Danville.

I remember making Pinewood Derby cars when Kevin was a Cub Scout and racing them against the other Cub Scouts.

I remember Kevin climbing trees as if he was Tarzan and leaping from rock to rock like a gazelle up here in Rock City in Mount Diablo, or on any number of hikes that we took up in Yosemite.

I remember Kevin smacking a triple in a come-from-behind win in a playoff game in Little League, and just a little later scoring the winning run by leaping into the air and stomping on home plate.

I remember as a family eating dinner, at sunset in Venice at a canalside trattoria that the gondoliers favored, and Kevin looked around and said, "I'm gonna propose in this place."

I remember walking our dog Chloe around the Woodranch neighborhood, and throwing a little rubber football around, and stopping to chat with the Tengs, or the Rivases or the Thompsons or the Grubaughs, who all live in that neighborhood.

I remember a triumphant high school graduate, last year in June 2017.

And more recently I remember meals at Mama's Fish House, on the north side of Maui, where we went once as a family, and where I had the good fortune of going twice with Kevin, just the two of us. Most recently was five weeks ago. It was a special day for both of us.

I could keep going through the mental photo album, but I want to be clear about one thing here today: We don't grieve for Kevin. Kevin is transformed. Kevin is in a place of perfect light and unconditional love. We do not grieve for Kevin. We grieve for ourselves, because our lives will have fewer examples of courage, grace, and dignity. In all those attributes, Kevin amazes me still.

So for ourselves, we may grieve. But Kevin would have us celebrate his amazing life and qualities. So let's talk about those qualities.

Kevin is—I'm going to use a lot of present tense here, because to some extent Kevin won't leave me or us—and maybe, because I'm also still in denial. So in present tense, Kevin is a stunningly handsome guy, and physically very strong. Along with his physical gifts, Kevin has a steely, fierce determination that made him a force to be reckoned with.

So I shared a little about Kevin's physical gifts, but he showed steel, both mental and physical, in all fields of athletics, for sure. But then his character would be tested in much tougher ways than sports. Cancer visited our family in December 2014. Through much of high school Kevin had surgeries, radiation treatments, and chemotherapy. He was bald for months at a time, often had little or no appetite, and was often just simply sick from the toxic chemo. He would miss a week of school at a time. Kevin had every excuse in the book not to graduate with his class. But he stayed after it, with that same grit and determination he showed on the sports field. We adjusted schedules, accommodated assignments, arranged tutors, and did summer classes. And at June 2017 I don't know that there was a prouder or happier graduate at San Ramon Valley High. And I can say for a fact that I know there were no prouder parents.

Kevin was just a freshman here at St. Mary's, so maybe his career was still some years off, but as a career he had his eye on international business. His love of travel and his skill with languages would have played well with that, I think. And I think his emerging maturity and self-knowledge would have made him effective with people. He and I got caught up recently with the re-airings of the Anthony Bourdain Parts Unknown *series. That was an effective way to "travel" and sample other cultures when real travel—or even leaving the house—became too challenging.*

Recently, Kevin also expressed an interest in becoming a support for or a mentor for young kids facing cancer treatments, sharing his experiences, and of course he would have immense empathy for and credibility with youngsters going through something like that.

Kevin didn't make friends with the ease that some people do. But he is fiercely loyal to the friends closest to him. He's among the most sensitive people I've ever encountered. If you only knew him on the surface, you would not pick this up. Kevin subdued his sensitivity. But a layer or two deeper, he picked up everything that was going on around him, and maybe not always to his own benefit. Marilene and I believe that he sometimes internalized things when he would have been better served to express them. This may even have been a factor in his illness.

So Kevin had many positive qualities. But we all have our negatives, as well. So sorry, buddy, but you're going to have to take a little medicine now. I can just hear him say, "Not more medicine *!!" Kevin, you are the most stubborn person I have ever met. You always have to have the last word. You didn't handle the word "No" well. And perhaps like most teenagers—maybe even like me at that age—you were of course never wrong. And of course you always knew more than we did. It's a funny thing about stubbornness, though. This stubbornness can rub people the wrong way. But Doctor Sallis, who's with us here today, thinks that that stubbornness was one of the reasons he was with us as long as he was. Stubbornness is perhaps a double-edged sword.*

But that said about stubbornness, Kevin was beginning to transform. He began to realize his own stubborn streak and began to see that stubbornness didn't always serve him or others well. He began to seek compromise, to reason and to negotiate. I wish he had more time to smooth out this rough edge in his spirit. But I am sure he is working on it with the help of some loving guides, where he is now.

Through three and a half years of cancer treatment Kevin almost never complained. In circumstances which would have buckled me at the knees, he simply said, "We'll get through it," or "What's the next treatment option?" Kevin was forced to learn lessons and grow in ways that many people only do when they age, if ever. Because of the determination and the grace with which he underwent all the treatments and discomforts, Kevin developed quite a bond with many people at UCSF over the last three years.

Kevin was just shy of twenty years old. He lived far more than some much older, and far less than his potential promised. What a force you

*would be, son. You literally shine with courage, grace, and dignity. I am
and will always be so proud of you. I am trying hard to be a father wor-
thy of your courage, but you set that bar pretty damn high, son.*

*Kevin, no Viking warrior ever fought more valiantly than you did or
earned a more glorious entry into Valhalla. I raise my mug to you, son.
Skol. And Godspeed.*

Thank you.

Reception

At the reception following the memorial service, various people came to
the microphone to share testimonials and anecdotes about Kevin. Two
stood out.

The first was from Claire, the girl Kevin loved. Claire read the text of an
e-mail from the English professor she and Kevin had shared, Professor
Thomas Cooney. Professor Cooney was traveling on the date of Kevin's
service. We asked Claire if she could read his e-mail because, quite
frankly, neither Marilene nor I thought we could get through it. Claire
read:

From: Thomas Cooney
To: Madsen Family
Date: July 3, 2018
Subject: Heartbroken

Dear Madsen Family:

*I just learned about Kevin's death, and though my grief is miniscule in
comparison to yours, you should know that Kevin left such an impression on me that I am struck with grief.*

Your son was a model student and person; the two are not often inter-changeable. I remember reading his final paper in late May, carrying with me a sense of how difficult his struggle has been. It was a good paper, not great, and my initial instinct was to give him an "A." But the Kevin I knew, the student, the fair, good and DECENT person, who WAS Kevin would have wanted the grade he earned, a "B." I hope that narrative speaks loudly enough to all of you exactly who Kevin was as a student.

As to who Kevin was as a person, I share this brief anecdote. One day in March I came to class a tad late. Kevin had missed the two previous classes and when I looked up to survey the room, my heart caught itself. There was Kevin, very frail, seated in his usual seat. I was so moved that I had to lie to the class and say I forgot something in my office, just so I could gather myself in the nearest bathroom. What so moved me was this: in that class were four of Kevin's friends who, like Kevin himself, also took me in the fall. Whether subconscious or not, they had gathered their chairs around him in such a manner that sent a message of love and protection. They weren't going to let anything happen to him in those 95 minutes. It's easy to disparage youth (I often do), but these five kids were angels, and Kevin himself was the saint they rallied around.

My deepest condolences and thoughts to all of you. My contribution would be minimal, but if there is anything I can do, please let me know. I am in Los Angeles until the 5th of July and then in Italy after July 16th.

My prayers to you all.

Thomas

The second speech which struck a tone came from Gustavo. Gus had not written anything for this. After a number of people had spoken, near the end of the reception, he stepped to the microphone.

Hi. I'm Gus. I think you all know me. I didn't come up here earlier be-cause I wanted to see you guys...and also because...I've had so many experiences with Kevin, if I tried to share them all it would take more time than we have. So I just came up here to share what I think would have been Kevin's one major piece of advice for me, for the rest of the time I have. And that would be...to just stop being a pussy.

This—coming as it did from a somewhat somber beginning—received the biggest laugh at the reception. And it tickled us all not only because of its inherent humor, but mainly because it was pure Kevin, to those who knew him. After the laughter tapered off, Gus continued.

He would tell me to stop being afraid of opportunities, meeting new people, new challenges. Stop being afraid of them. What else? Somebody else said it. When he was going through cancer treatment three times, he would just say, "What's next?" And that's part of what "stop being a pussy" means. Just stop wondering why stuff is happening to you, and get it done.

Kevin...I was actually amazed at how people reacted to Kevin sometimes. Because, to me sometimes he could be a...pretty big ass {more laughter}. He was my big brother. And you do little brother things, and sometimes it offends. Trent here had a nickname from Kevin that ...I'll just give the initials...P.N.B. {Pause} Pussy No Balls. {More laughter} He was joking around with people, a lot of times more than I would like. I was astonished because Trent, Nick, Will...all of my friends ...they were always telling me how much they loved him and how much they enjoyed being around him and I was always like {here, Gus makes an exaggerated "Are You Kidding Me?" look on his face, to more laughter}.

And I think that just kinda speaks to how he didn't view that he had to explain why he liked you or why he wanted to spend time around you. His love for all of you guys was just implied...he just had this capacity to immediately accept people and that's taken me a while to understand, actually....Long time. Even to this day, I think there's a lot of people here that just had no idea how much he loved you.

I'll leave you guys with that.

Those were just two of a number of warm, insightful, and funny testimonials offered throughout the reception.

After all the speeches concluded, people milled around, talked, ate the food staged on the various tables, sipped their drinks, and perused all the exhibits of photos of Kevin and the family, from his infancy to young man. I needed to be by myself, so I stepped outside the hall and into a nearby garden. Finding a chair in a tucked-away corner of this garden, near a hedge, I sat. I sat for several minutes, elbows on knees, head in hands.

My head still down, I hadn't noticed that Gus had silently walked over and now stood next to me.

"Dad," he began, "I think Kevin is beaming." Gus went on to say that he didn't see how the service and the reception could have gone better.

I stood, put my arm around Gus's shoulder, and we turned to walk back into the hall.

"I'm glad you think so, son." I replied. "He deserves it."

Despair

Grief hung like sandbags from my shoulders. I rose from bed out of grim obligation, and for no other reason. The simple now seemed insurmountable; the mundane turned into mountains. Chewing and swallowing required so much effort as to almost cramp my jaw, and for food with no taste. The grape had gone out of the wine. Hot water melted with hot tears, the hashy sound of the spray almost covering my sobs there on the shower floor. Could others see the hole through my middle? I felt that there was nothing there.

Forced out of the house to resupply, I dimmed the lights in each aisle of the supermarket, lying to the checkout clerk when they asked me how my day was going.

Marilene cried every day, often several times a day. I tried to comfort her, but I so often felt that I could not make the slightest dent in her misery, and then I felt guilty about *that*.

Signs

Four days after Kevin passed, we found a small owl up in the rafters of the gazebo which adjoins the deck in our back yard. The gazebo has a small table and two chairs. We sat there for half an hour. The little owl—maybe six inches in height—perched only four or five feet above us, made no effort to fly off, only slightly turning his head this way and that, whenever we moved about below. He seemed quite comfortable and content to remain. Finally, we had other things to do, and had to leave. The owl was still there when we left.

A couple days after the owl, Marilene called me over to her, when she stood at the kitchen sink. She pointed out the kitchen window. At first, I didn't know what she meant or see what she pointed at. Then I saw it.

Marilene's car—a black GMC Terrain—sat parked in our driveway, just outside the kitchen window. At the very tip of the antenna on her car perched a dragonfly the color of red-orange flame.

We each went outside, stood near the car, watched and spoke to the beautiful visitor. After ten minutes, it flew off. But within a minute it seemed to complete an aerial lap of the house, and it returned to the exact same spot, perched facing in the exact same direction on that antenna. After another ten-minute stay, the creature repeated the exact same dance, lapping the house, returning to its perch, and once more facing in exactly the same direction.

This happened six straight times. Each time, the dragonfly spent about ten minutes perched, took a one-minute or less circuit of the house, and returned to its perch, every time faced in exactly the same direction.

In some Asian and Native American cultures, dragonflies are a symbol of transformation.

Hannah

A couple weeks after Kevin's service, we had a visit. Kevin's good friend Hannah—along with her mother—came by our house. Hannah and her family had been in Hawaii when Kevin passed, and they hadn't returned in time for the service. Hannah was heartbroken that she couldn't be there.

On the same day as the service, while they were still in Hawaii, Hannah made a point of going to a church and offering some prayers. Later, making a lei from braided seaweed and roses, she took it to the beach. There, she drew "Kev" in the sand, formed the lei in the shape of a heart around his name, and let the waves come in and take the lei.

That same afternoon, Hannah's family took a hike on a trail through the rain forest. At a pause on the hike, they noticed that they were being followed by a group of twenty or so dragonflies. When they stopped, the dragonflies stopped.

Hannah's mother said, "Hannah, Kevin's sending them."

Neither Hannah nor her mom had heard anything about our experience a couple weeks before with the brilliant flame-orange dragonfly outside our house.

Brazil, August 2018

Eight months after his last visit to Brazil, Kevin returned; this time, for good.

Among all the agonizing decisions and tasks we had to complete that summer, one decision we were able to make without hesitation. We would bury Kevin's ashes in the family mausoleum in Paraguassu in Brazil, next to his grandparents Mozart and Lourdes. We wanted it, and we knew that Kevin would want it.

Our Brazilian family—mainly Marilene's sisters Marina and Marcia— had arranged a memorial service at a spot Kevin and Gustavo loved to visit many times over the years during our visits to Brazil. Vale das Pedras (Valley of Stones) is an eco-tourism inn on the banks of the Rio Sapucai just seven kilometers from Paraguassu. Rio Sapucai blends the Portuguese Rio (River) with the name Sapucai (SAP-oo-kah-EE). Sapucai comes from the indigenous language Tupi Guarani. Together, Rio Sapucai translates as "river which sings."

There at Vale das Pedras, two rivers merge and generate mild rapids which splash over boulders and rocky banks. The owners of the inn took care to preserve as much as possible of the plant and tree life on their side of the river. Sometimes, on the opposite bank, you can catch a glimpse of a family of capybara.

From when the boys were as young as four and five years old, they had always clamored to visit Vale das Pedras on every trip. They loved to explore two low, rocky peninsulas which jut out into the river. Kevin especially loved going out to the very farthest points of these peninsulas, where the current is strongest, as he was always very comfortable with hiking over rocks.

A small island sat close to the banks of the river, near the inn. The owners had linked the island to their property with an Indiana Jones-style rope-and-wood-plank suspension bridge. The game there, of course, was to bounce the bridge when your brother was on it, trying to bounce him off or scare him. Rope swings hang from a handful of trees near the river, one of which swings out over the river itself, irresistible to young boys.

The inn has a main dining hall, overlooking the river, which serves buffet meals to inn guests and visitors. Just outside the dining hall, a half-dozen open thatched-roof huts with wood tables and benches invite you to sit, chat, eat, and drink. In good weather, we've spent hours over many pleasant meals at those tables, sipping ice-cold cerveja(which keeps getting replenished!) or Guarana, the national soft drink of Brazil, made from berries sourced from the Amazon, and at one time more popular than Coca-Cola), eating fresh fish with *batatas fritas* (french fries), or various other fresh and tasty finger foods. The inn at one time had regular visits from a monogamous pair of toucans which became fairly tame and accustomed to people. At one time we had a photo of a smiling Kevin, exchanging glances with one of these toucans perched on his shoulder.

On the day of the memorial for Kevin at Vale das Pedras, about eighty people gathered outside about fifty meters from the riverbank, under a large broad pergola which shaded a flat area set with some tables and chairs. Our good friends Cesario and Valeria read some prayers, and Marilene and I shared some emotional testimonials in Portuguese. Some of the family also shared impromptu thoughts and stories. One of the most notable came from our nephew Caio, now a doctor and himself a survivor of testicular cancer some ten years ago. Caio had been visiting us just a few weeks before, over Gustavo's graduation, and he saw what we were going through. He shared a testimonial on the love and warmth in our family, and on Kevin's courage.

When all the speeches were done, and people milled around chatting, I walked off to be alone with my thoughts, and with Kevin. I wandered over to one of the rope swings. The swing had a seat tied to the end of the rope, formed from a branch two feet long and two inches thick. I clutched the wood of the seat, smoothed by years of rides, the memories coming thick and fast. The boys—one at a time, of course—used to straddle that branch, the rope up between their legs and their hands gripping the rope at head-height, grins already locked-in. Then I would grip either end of the seat-branch, walk them away from the river fifteen or so feet, until my arms clutching the seat-branch reached as high above my head as they would go. Anticipation peaked ("Go, Dad! Go!"), I would hold them there in suspense a moment, before running with as much speed as I could muster toward the river. At my point of no return, I gave an extra thrust with my arms and propelled them into space, out over the river as much as twenty feet away from the bank and fifteen feet over the water. In mock-fear but undisguised glee, at the height of their flight they would shout "Whooooa!" As they swung back over the bank at some speed, I would grab their shoulders, or the seat-branch, whatever I could, saying as I ran with them once more, "I'm gonna launch you offa this thing!" and propel them even higher on the next pendulum-swing ("Higher, Dad! Higher!"). It never got old. The only thing which ended a turn was a waiting brother, or, finally, after half an hour or forty-five minutes, Dad's fatigue.

My eyes brimming with the memory, I gripped where the knot was tied just above the center of the seat-branch and flung it, with all I had, out over the river and into the sky.

The next day, at the town cemetery, where twenty years before I had first seen all the Prado and Silva names on the various memorials, we met the funeral director. We brought Kevin's ashes in the small case from the matched luggage he bought just two days before he passed, the luggage that he had told Marilene, "We're gonna need it." The container we were given from the crematory exactly fit into the small case, with almost no room to spare at top, bottom, or either side.

We wanted this to be a small group. The only people present were me, Marilene, Gustavo, Gustavo's friend Nick Zabaneh from California, and Marilene's sister Marina who came from work on her lunch break, and the funeral director.

After a brief prayer, we walked from the velatorium over to the gravesite, where a chamber in the family vault had been opened. The granite slab which had covered the opening leaned against a stone nearby, and twenty or so bricks were stacked at the ready. Gustavo asked for a few minutes with Kevin's case. Sniffing, murmuring a few things, and cradling the case in his left hand, while running the fingertips of his right hand over its surface, Gus said his goodbyes. We each placed a kiss on the case.

Finally, I placed the case into the chamber. The worker mixed some water into a mound of dry, powdery mortar, then mixed and worked the mortar with his trowel. Then, as we watched, he slapped down a layer of gray wet mortar at the lip of the open chamber, smoothing it with the trowel. One by one, he laid in three bricks, tapping each into place with the handle of his trowel, scraping off the excess mortar which had squeezed out between the bricks, and then troweled on some more mortar on top. Wordlessly, methodically, he troweled and stacked and scraped. Soon, he was left with a small hole into which he mortared-in a final half-brick, and then set about scraping off the remaining excess mortar. My breath caught as he set that last half-brick in place, and I hung my head. I thought I had already reckoned with the finality of all of it. But the rawness had not begun to scab over.

The worker retrieved the granite slab which would cover the brickwork. With a little mortar as glue, and a few taps from a rubber mallet, he sealed the vault shut.

A Lighter Moment

A few weeks after returning from Brazil, which was about eighty days since Kevin passed, Gustavo, Marilene and I each tackled tasks for dinner preparation one evening. In the middle of it, Gustavo paused to link his phone to our television audio system, and he began to play some music from one of his Spotify playlists. Gus has diverse taste in music. He enjoys everything from Brazilian popular and country music, to funk and Motown classics (gets that from me), to jazz, rock, and reggae, on which he and Kevin both got indoctrinated on our first trip to Maui.

Soon after he cued his playlist, one of my favorite Al Green tunes, "Love and Happiness," came on. The song starts with an unmistakable soulful guitar breakdown, before a gospel-like keyboard joins in.

"Oh, man!" I enthused. "It don't get no bettah than *this*!" Gus and I grinned at each other, as he remotely dialed up the volume a bit. Marilene smiled and continued chopping something on the countertop. I started to do a few *Soul Train* dance moves.

It was the lightest moment in the house since Kevin passed, more than two months before. We all felt it. A moment like this seemed a long, long way off even the week before.

"Look," Marilene said. Gus and I followed her gaze. She stared at the box window above the kitchen sink, which overlooks the front of our house, out to the street. A couple weeks after Kevin's passing, a friend who had heard the story of our orange dragonfly sighting had given Marilene a stained-glass dragonfly ornament. This piece is about four inches long and four inches wide, with a red body and clear wings. We had hung it with clear nylon fishing line from a white metal rack in the box window, a rack probably intended for potted plants.

The stained-glass dragonfly was swinging side to side, "wagging" its tail, about a third of an inch to either side of center when still. We all watched for several seconds; it showed no signs of slowing.

"He's happy that we're happy," Marilene noted, in a muted, thoughtful voice, a knowing smile on her face.

When she first pointed this out, Marilene was ten feet from that box window. We never open that window, so it is never open to the outside air, nor are there any vents or other sources of moving air near it. And that stained-glass dragonfly had not ever moved before this, nor has it once moved in the fifteen months since.

Therapy

In those black days after Kevin passed, a couple of things took me out of myself. Chores was one. Nature was another.

At home I marinated in misery. Shut indoors, maybe it's instinctual, maybe it's the nesting gene, but you breathe and re-breathe the same sad air, you play and replay the same sad scenes. Marilene and I hugged a lot, and cried together, and grieved over the photos from the service, the array of photos that celebrated the life of our son, the Lion. Television, grocery shopping, or our smartphones distracted us briefly, but were like paper bridges over deep gray water; at any moment we might tumble in. Once the movie was done, or the groceries stashed, we were once more faced with an idle moment and a deep well, waiting to be dipped. Grief hovered constantly, patiently, arms folded, puppet strings relaxed but poised, knowing that He would soon enough jerk from us convulsed, wracking sobs.

Idleness fermented grief, slowing time, stretching hours out, sapping energy like a withering flame when a jar is placed over the candle, consuming the oxygen trapped there. To ward off idleness, I attacked the trees surrounding the deck at the back of the house.

Fast-growing bay trees had pinched off part of the view from our back deck. Over the course of a couple days, I pruned them way back. The close-in stuff was not difficult with regular pruning shears. But many of the branches were fifteen or more feet out. I had to use pole-shears to reach those. The work forced some awkward stretches, reaches, and contortions. After cutting several hundred branches over two days, I was sore all over. But I had the satisfaction of seeing results; our view was much improved.

Chores were therapeutic, but nature transformed us. We moved from the stale air to the fresh, from the confined, roofed space to the open. And not only being *out* in the open, but *being* open. Soaking up our surroundings as observers, not actors. Breathing, slowly letting wonder seep in, infusing our senses, tickling and tingling all, down to our cell walls. And when you open and make yourself available to nature, She performs, and things begin to happen. A dragonfly does you a dance. A red-tailed hawk glides low near you, and the low, late-afternoon winter sun lights up its tail like polished copper. A praying mantis shows up in your bedroom, in a place not known for praying mantises. A tree branch shudders and its leaves clatter in still air, when none of the trees or branches nearby move at all. A succession of rainbows parades across your view; one even follows you on a road trip. Flocks of pelicans glide past the sea cliff moving north from left to right; a series of them, twenty to a group, half a dozen groups. One pelican makes a U turn, as if to collect stragglers. As you watch the pelicans, a movement on the ocean nearby catches your eye: humpback whales, heading south.

Slowly, a feeling comes over you. Or perhaps better said, it wells up within you. You begin to realize that there's more going on here than you as distinct and dispassionate observer, passing by a movable screen. No, pay attention. What is that? Your senses balloon away out from your body, expanding, embracing all around you. That tingle just behind your forehead? More than your physical five senses are at play here. And it is play, isn't it? More than dialogue, it is dance, it is song. It feels like—it has the vibration of—a warm *invitation*. Sponge-like, you invite a magical flow of energy into your sphere. A hummingbird flits about nearby. But it is not feeding, nor does it seem to be sniffing out flowers or buds. The bird circles, zig-zags, dives, and climbs, for a full minute, without lighting on a tree branch or sipping at a bud. Wait a minute...you say to yourself—or whoever is listening—in your mind...*Was that for me?! Of course it was.* Did I just "hear" that?! Allow the wonder. Trust it. Invite the delight, molting-off the "adult" dead skin and kicking it off to the side of the trail. And when Nature senses that *you* sense it, in shared delight now, the flirtations, dances, and songs escalate to another level, like electrons climbing to the higher-energy shell in the atom.

I got so that when stepping out my front door, the envelope of my senses popped out to the horizon and to the sky and clouds above. What was there for me? It had been available to me all along, and I'd always corralled my field of view to a narrow swath just before me and to either side. What a waste! How *could* I have closed myself off from so much!? But I am open to it now, all senses firing. And it comes rushing in, a delighted shower of electric color, crystalline light, sound and sensation. And somewhere at the center, I become aware of a release, a letting-go.

If I stay still and alert, I feel that it all hums. All of it: the air, the earth, the trees. And I am immersed in it. And the same hum runs through me.

Turning a Corner

In September 2018, just three months after Kevin passed, Marilene and I sat out on the back deck, drinking coffee. I was scanning the news on my phone. Marilene was shopping on hers. Only she was not shopping on Amazon. She was seeking a comedy club act in the hopes of making it a gift to Gustavo for his birthday in October. Her idea was to send Gus and five friends to a comedy show, then to dinner in North Beach, the traditional Italian neighborhood in San Francisco. I liked her idea.

Marilene scanned the shows at Cobb's Comedy Club, where we had been recently for a show, in an effort to break us out of our funk. Cobb's is adjacent to North Beach, so convenient for the brainstormed birthday outing for Gus. As it turned out, the Gustavo birthday idea never crystallized, but something much better—something transforming—came out of the search.

As she scanned through the Cobb's website for October comedy acts, she stumbled onto something else. On one mid-October Saturday afternoon at 3:00, Cobb's was offering a show with Bill Philipps, a psychic medium. This tickled her curiosity. Philipps has a website of his own. Marilene pulled it up, and we perused it for several minutes. The tickets were not expensive, only $25 each. So we agreed, "Why not?" and pulled the trigger and bought two tickets.

Leading up to the date of the show, it was hard not to get our hopes up. We knew that there would be a club full of people. Equally, we knew that there was simply no way, during a maybe two-hour show, that Philipps could get around to everyone there. So we went there knowing that he might not even speak to us, but hoping that we might get *some* small sign or message that Kevin was okay. I have told many people since that "my expectations were here…" holding my hand flat and level, three inches above the table, "…my hopes were here…" raising my hand to six inches above the table, "…and what happened was here!" my hand raised over my head.

As the day for the show grew near, I got increasingly anxious. The tension between what I hoped for and what I knew was likely drew a knot in my chest, tighter and tighter the closer the day approached.

On the morning before the show, I took Chloe for a walk. I looked up in the blue sky and I spoke to Kevin, imploring him to come to us, begging him to come through with a message for us at the show the next afternoon.

I also want to say that, while I asked for and hoped for Kevin's presence, I approached the show with what I'd like to think was a healthy dose of skepticism. I believed that legitimate mediumship existed out there somewhere. But I also knew that there were numerous frauds. And I didn't know Philipps from Adam; he could be the real deal, or he could be a complete sham. I tried to imagine, "If I were faking such a show, how would I do it?" I might have "plants" in the audience, with scripted stories that Philipps would cue and that the plants would validate, maybe crying for good measure. I would look at the last names of all the ticket buyers and research on the internet recent passings with those last names, try to link them up. And I suppose there could be much on the web that would make for a good show, again, if I were faking it. In that spirit of healthy skepticism, I resolved that I wasn't going to easily give up too much information to Philipps. I was going to make him *work* for this one!

Bill Philipps was younger than I expected, in his mid-thirties. At the show's outset, he explained that his mother had passed when he was fourteen. She came to him in a dream the next night. She told him that he had untapped abilities, that she would help him develop those abilities in order to help others. He has been on a mission almost ever since, after first dabbling—successfully—as an opera singer!

The club had about 100 people in it when the show began at 3:00 on Saturday, October 13, 2018. Philipps began with a meditation, where we all imagined a bright light coming down from the heavens into the crown of our heads, and cascading from there down and throughout our bodies.

He explained how these readings go. Messages can seem quite random and can "bounce" from one side of the room to the other. He gets messages from the other side and then prompts the crowd to see if that message has meaning for anyone. An audience member "validates" by raising a hand. He said that once he begins a show, and "opens the door," the folks from the other side crowd in and all are trying to jam in their message, so it can get tricky for him to weed through all the traffic! He further explained that when he gets words or names or numbers, it can "sound" as if he's getting noise underwater. So "Helen" can sound like "Ellen," or "Evan" like "Kevin." Finally, he mentioned that messages received today may not even click until days, weeks, even years away. For the people on the other side, time does not exist. Or, said differently, time is *all now.*

When the preliminaries were done, and Philipps began to read, some of the first things he threw out to the audience were "Tom" and "Joey." I raised my hand and he called on me. Did either of those names mean anything to me, he asked? "Yeah, my name is Tom," I of course replied. But he said he was after a recently departed Tom, so he kind of waved me off and moved on to others in the audience.

He read for a handful of folks. Some were quite moved by his insights. A woman seated twenty feet from us was moved to tears by his description of and insights on her grandfather. It all seemed quite genuine.

He said he was getting "27" and did that mean anything to anyone? No one seemed to click on that one, so he moved on. Marilene tapped me on the elbow and whispered, "The 27th was the day Kevin passed!" Oh ! Of course!

By the time Marilene and I realized the significance of 27, Philipps was in the middle of reading for other people, so I had to sit tight for a few minutes. When he finished with them, he asked the audience as a whole "Are there any questions on all this so far?" So I thrust my hand in the air so he wouldn't miss it.

"A few minutes ago you mentioned '27,'" I said. "It didn't click at first, but my wife and I realized that that was the date our son passed."

And so began an eight-minute riff on Kevin and on us. Philipps crossed the stage to a point closest to our table in the club. He began....

"You have two sons." This was a statement, not a question. We nodded in validation.

"I'm getting a hard 'C' sound as a start to the name," he continued.

"Kevin," we acknowledged. I decided to give him that one.

Philipps went on. "He's with the teachers, he says. Does that make any sense?"

I answered, "Both my parents were teachers, and my wife's mother was also a teacher."

Philipps continued. "I'm getting a 'Dan' or a 'Don,' does that resonate? I'm getting a 'D' and an 'N,'"

No, we replied, that doesn't ring a bell.

"Now I'm getting a guitar," Philipps continued.

"Dylan!" we both exclaimed together. "That's it!" said Philipps. Dylan was Kevin's closest friend his freshman year at St. Mary's College. Kevin and Dylan were planning to room together their sophomore year. Dylan is a fairly accomplished musician. He has taught music and been paid for it, has written some of his own stuff, and has even dabbled in performing publicly.

"Kevin said that Dylan should continue with his music," offered Philipps. "Kevin said he's sorry he missed the celebration." We were initially puzzled, but finally agreed that he was referring to his 20th birthday, which he missed by just one month when he passed. "He also wants you to know he apologizes for being such a burden."

Bill Philipps had not been told how Kevin passed, but this message— with my skeptic hat on—could have been pieced together from information out there in the public domain, such as on the CaringBridge website, *if* someone had the time and resources to research it. When I heard the "burden" thing, I immediately thought it meant that Kevin was sorry we had been forced to make the decision to pull the breathing tube at the hospital. Marilene's take was that he was sorry for the last several months, when Kevin required almost 24-hour care. So here was Kevin apologizing to us, and I had for four months been hoping / wondering if Kevin could forgive *me* for deciding to pull that tube!

"He wants you to know that he's breathing easily now, running and jumping. He has new athletic shoes." Kevin was naturally athletic and graceful, effortlessly and fearlessly climbing trees or bounding over boulders. During his last month, his breathing became increasingly labored, to the point that climbing one flight of stairs had his heart pounding. And, of course, his last hours were spent with that breathing tube down his throat.

"Kevin says thank you for the donation you made in his name."

This didn't click for me and Marilene in the moment. The way that Philipps worded it, we thought it meant a monetary donation. We hadn't made any large monetary donations to anything, so we scratched our heads on that one. But later, after the show, we remembered the donation of his corneas, which had given two other people sight! In addition, we had donated his tumor tissue for research purposes. So Philipps' comment made sense, after all.

Three times I thought Philipps was wrapping up with us and getting ready to move on to others. In fact, I grew a little self-conscious, because there were so many in the audience that I knew would not get anything. I began to imagine jealous stares drilling into the back of my head from the crowd around us. But each time I thought he was moving on from us, he got another scrap of message from Kevin! I now think that Kevin must have been quite insistent.

Philipps went on, now addressing me. "Are you writing something? A journal, maybe?"

I had been writing for some weeks, mostly about our grief. So I acknowledged that yes, I had been writing.

Philipps said, and with notable certainty, "Kevin's helping you with that. He wants you to keep writing."

Marilene and I both felt numbed, but buoyant, about how much was coming across that resonated so strongly of Kevin. Philipps now turned his attention to her.

"He says you have his necklace," he directed to Marilene.

Marilene had a blouse with a high neckline, and no necklace showing. She placed a hand over her collarbone, feeling for something, but had a puzzled look on her face. In her mind, she was guessing that Philipps could have been referring to a cross that Kevin wore on a silver chain. But she did not have it on her at the time, nor did she ever wear it. So in the moment, at the show, this point from Philipps did not really resonate.

Note: The next day, when Marilene changed out of her pajamas to get ready to go out, she looked in the mirror. Suddenly, "my necklace" made sense! Around her neck was the gold chain and the dragonfly pendant that her sister Marcia had given her. That chain had been under her blouse when we were at Philipps's show, but the chain is so fine and the pendant so thin that she hadn't felt it when she raised her hand to her throat, and she had been focused on necklaces that Kevin had actually worn. The significance to us of the dragonfly is covered at length elsewhere. A day after we were elated at inescapable proof that Kevin was "talking" to us, one more message and point of validation came to us that morning!

Philipps said, "I'm getting a photo in a frame. Kevin waving a flag."

This was the clincher moment, the moment when any remaining doubt just evaporated. On our wall at home, we have a framed picture of Kevin, given to us by the mother of one of Kevin's close friends from high school. The photo was taken July 4, 2017, near the end of Kevin's treatment for his second cancer, and a few months before we discovered his third. The image is of Kevin, body sideways to the camera, but face turned toward the lens. He is in the middle of one of the suburban streets in our old neighborhood, on a street which slopes slightly uphill. Kevin's right foot is on his skateboard, his left is planted on the asphalt. Raised in his right fist is a pole carrying a full-size American flag, curled in the breeze almost like the famous Iwo Jima flag. And his face looks triumphant, his mouth wide open as if he's roaring like a lion.

"That's how he wants to be remembered," added Philipps.

Marilene and I both had to wipe our eyes at that one. I felt Kevin then, loud and clear. It was him, of that I have no doubt, anymore.

"I'm getting a dog. Is it Joey? Zoe?" asked Philipps. Chills. "Chloe," we acknowledged, remembering the "sounds underwater" caution from the beginning.

"That's it!" said Philipps. "He's playing with her." Chloe has since left us. She had golden-brown spots above each eye. We were told once that the Navajo believe that such dogs can see spirits.

"Kevin says he is helping other kids who've passed tragically. He's helping them with their transitions."

Again, tears. A few months before he passed, Kevin was asked by a spiritual coach what he would like to do in life. Kevin replied that he felt he could take what he had learned from his cancer experience and help young kids.

As Philipps wrapped up his show forty-five minutes later, Marilene excused herself to go to the ladies' room before we left. On the way there, a middle-aged woman came up to her, gave her a hug, and told Marilene that she was so happy for us, for how much we had received from Kevin, through Philipps.

We left transformed. We immediately walked over a few blocks to a traditional Italian restaurant. We needed to sit down and capture all we had heard in the show, before we forgot it. In fact, we counted twenty-two items or signs from the show; I've listed only the most impactful ones here. We had thrown a dart at a psychic medium show and had hit the bullseye and the lottery in one throw.

I remembered the ask that I had made of Kevin, the one during the morning walk with Chloe. As Marilene and I tucked into our pasta and sipped some wine, a new image formed. I felt Kevin, responding—with insistence and urgency—to my request. Not only that, but I could almost see him elbowing his way through to the front of the "line" of spirits who wanted to get through to someone in that audience. So, not only did the *information* shared in the show prove to us that Kevin was in touch with us, and okay, but the *way* in which it came across was pure Kevin, as well, like the time when he tucked the rugby ball under his arm and broke six tackles as he ran upfield.

It's one thing to hope for and believe in something, and we still would have, even if we hadn't had any interaction with Bill Philipps that day. It's another thing entirely to see and feel your beliefs validated, beyond doubt, in a way so personal as to be irrefutable, and with so much love. And to *know* that your loved one carries on and watches over you, and that we all carry on, when the time comes, is to change your outlook completely, and there's no returning to the former you. And nor would you want to return to the former you, because you're now wrapped in a comfort like you've never known.

We made our way home happy, for the first time in a very long time.

Lost and Found

Kevin was not happy with Marilene.

Four months after he had passed, we had immersed ourselves in cleaning up our back yard. Some context is in order. Our house in Walnut

Creek is built on the lip of a hill. This hill drops off dramatically behind and beneath the deck at the back of the house. It slopes so much that you have to fight to keep your feet when walking across it. The property at the bottom backs onto a regional park. With the steep slope and no houses below or behind us, we enjoy sweeping views from our back deck.

In October 2018, a year's worth of dead leaves had accumulated on this slope. Of course, California has suffered some horrific fires the last couple years. Also, our homeowner's association rules mandated that our properties needed to be regularly cleared of such debris. But rules or no rules, there was simply too much fuel on the ground. So we could pay gardeners a lot to clean it up, or we could attempt it ourselves. Four months after Kevin's death, we remained in a funk. Marilene and I felt that the exertion would do us good, so we opted to attack it ourselves.

We decked out in boots, hats and gloves, grabbed rakes, shovels, water bottles, and 30-gallon plastic leaf bags, and began working our way down the slope, raking down as we went, and pausing when we had large piles of leaves which we shoveled into bags. We could do this for only a couple hours at a go; the work was physical, dirty. The toughest parts were maintaining balance on the extreme slope and trudging 30-pound bags back up that slope to the house. The "yard"—really it's more like a park or forest—would take weeks to complete, there was so much of it.

We slipped and fell on our butts a number of times. You couldn't avoid it on that steep slope. Not only is it steep, but the footing is poor, and we wore rubber boots most of the time, to prevent spiders climbing up under our jeans. Marilene feared snakes.

A couple of weeks into this effort, we had cleared about half the property of loose leaves. Good therapy. After a couple hours of this, we would be exhausted, sweaty, dirty. After a hot shower and a change to fresh clothes, we would be renewed. Late one afternoon, we worked on different sides of the property. I couldn't see Marilene through the trees, but we kept track of each other by shouting. She slipped, took a tumble onto her butt, and slid somewhat down the hill. But she popped right back up, brushed herself off after first checking for snakes, climbed back up to where she had been working, and resumed.

The afternoon was getting on, and the sun sets early that time of year, so we stopped raking and lugged heavy bags of leaves back up to the house. We staged the bags on a patio that abuts the back of our garage. As Marilene crossed that patio by a back door to the garage, she reached into her back pocket for her smartphone. Just at that moment, she heard a clatter sound from behind the closed door to the garage. Odd. We were the only people at home; Gustavo was out. Smartphone not where she thought. What was that noise? She opened the back door to the garage.

There, on the floor of the garage, was a framed 8 x 10 photo of Kevin in his #57 varsity football uniform. We had had it displayed on a shelf at eye level in the garage, along with dozens of other photos from the memorial service. Basically, a whole quadrant of the garage is now a shrine to Kevin. The photo—which has a glass facing protecting the image—had fallen from eye level down to the cement garage floor and had ended up about eight feet into the garage—that is, away from the shelf from which it had fallen. That was the clatter Marilene had heard, without doubt. The glass was unbroken; noteworthy, for the height of the fall, as well as for how far into the garage it ended up.

Marilene replaced the photo carefully up on its shelf. She scoured the house for her phone.

I declared victory over the last two leafbags of the day and threw them down on the patio backing the garage, just as Marilene emerged from the house.

"I think I lost my cellphone down there," she said. "It was in my back pocket. I slipped and fell. It must have fallen out."

I thought one thing, but said another. What I *thought* was: *Honey, how could you carry your phone there in all this debris, on that hairy slope, and in your back pocket?!* What I *said* was: "Ahhh, don't worry, baby, we'll find it."

Then, Marilene shared with me that Kevin's framed photo in the garage had fallen. Happily, it wasn't broken. She mentioned that she had heard the noise in the garage just as she had realized her phone wasn't in her back pocket.

Okaaaaaaaayyyy.......

I need to explain something here. When Kevin died, Marilene couldn't bear to part with his smartphone. So she had the SIM card transferred from her old smartphone to Kevin's. She had adopted Kevin's phone. The wallpaper you see when you turn on this phone is a sweet photo of Kevin's face, right next to his Mom's, both smiling warmly into the camera.

So no, Kevin wasn't happy with Marilene in that moment. And this display of irritation—the photo falling off the shelf—was exactly in-character.

Marilene—understandably—was desperate to find that phone. We returned to the area she was working when she fell. I called her number from my phone, in the hopes we would hear it ring or see the screen light up. But her phone was in silent mode. It was getting dark, so we might have gotten lucky and seen the screen light up. But if the phone was face down or lay beneath several inches of dead leaves, our chances were poor. I called and called and called that number. Marilene scoured several hundred square feet of slope, as best she could in the growing darkness. But no luck.

By the time it got full dark, it was pointless at least for that day to try to find that phone. Marilene persisted maybe twenty minutes longer. I finally persuaded her that we would return in daylight and that I was sure we would find it then. I hoped that my voice was more persuasive than I felt.

That night I asked Kevin to help us find the phone the next day.

So the next day we re-outfitted and together scoured the slope in the area Marilene fell the day before. In my mind, I once more implored Kevin for his help.

We raked, bagged, and stepped. As I bagged leaves I carefully mined through the debris, looking for the phone. We raked, sifted, and bagged, carefully, for half an hour. We both bent over our work, maybe twenty feet apart.

I stood briefly, to ease my back and take a moment's break. Just then, a large blue jay flew into a low branch of a tree just twenty feet to my left. The jay began screeching up a storm. I mean it was *loud.* I watched it for about a minute. It kept up an extremely loud screech throughout. As I regarded the bird, the word *insistent* came to mind.

"Honey, when I finish this bag, I'm gonna go over where that blue jay is putting up a fuss. Maybe he knows something!" I said to Marilene.

She said, "Sure. Who knows?"

I bent back down to my work. I scooped up in my gloves a double handful of leaves, feeling through them for a solid object like a phone as I bagged them. Something slid down the hill into the spot from which I had just scooped.

It was Marilene's (Kevin's) phone, a little dusty but none the worse for wear.

I stopped, brushed off the dust from the phone, held it up in Marilene's direction, and waited for her to realize I had stopped. Immersed in her work, she didn't notice me at all. I waited a couple minutes. So finally I said, "Hey."

Marilene turned, saw what I held in my hand, and beamed as she trudged toward me in her boots. "You *found* it!" she enthused. She hugged and kissed me.

"Well, *someone* did," I replied.

Grief Support

Four months after Kevin passed, Marilene and I joined a Parents Grief Group, run out of the Contra Costa Crisis Center near our home. Everyone in this group had lost a son or a daughter. One woman lost both a son *and* a daughter, less than a month apart! The group is led and facilitated by two men, each of whom had also lost a son years before. The group meets at a conference room in the CCCC each Wednesday from 7-9 p.m.

From November 2018 to June 2019 this group helped us more than we could have imagined. It's not that there is some magic switch that's flipped and the fog-mist of grief evaporates. No, there's no such relief, I'm afraid. But what it *does* offer is the perspective of others who are going through what you are. It surprised me how therapeutic that was. No one else can begin to fathom what you're feeling. Perfectly well-meaning people say things like "I just can't imagine..." or "I lost my father last year..." or even "I lost my dog...." Now, grief is a very personal, a very individual, experience. Perhaps it's nearly as individual as fingerprints or snowflakes. And there may not be one "right" way to get through grief, no timeline, no formula. But please believe me when I say that losing a parent or a dog cannot compare with losing a child of any age. We all bury our parents. There's a warp in the universe when we bury a child.

Anyhow, we began our first session with the grief group by saying our child's name, and then sharing briefly how our child passed. An electronic candle sat on the floor in the middle of the circle, and Kleenex boxes were within reach. After the introductions, the format of the group just opens up to discuss whatever someone wants to share or ask. Some themes have included: What have you found useful easing your grief? How are you memorializing your child? How do you persuade others not to forget your child? How do you deal with guilt?

As we came to know the people and the stories in our group, we found that three other sets of parents had lost sons in the same month we lost Kevin, and all were around the same age. In the broader group, the causes of loss ran the spectrum: accidents, cancers, drug overdoses, congenital heart defects—and there were a couple of suicides, too.

The group numbered as high as eighteen people on some weeks, around twelve to fifteen usually. Some parents came in couples. Others came solo. With some of the couples, you could make out pretty quickly that the two of them were in very different places with their grief. Perhaps the mother was still despondent, even years after the death, while the father stoically compartmentalized his grief and kept his head down, immersed in work. It seemed to me in some cases that bottled grief manifested in physical ways, in pains or illnesses.

The first four months with this group surprised me. I got so that I looked forward to Wednesday evenings, to be with the group, to hear their stories and share ours, to support each other, and to share with people who *understood* what we were going through, as no one else could, even with the best of intentions. I think the rhythm of it worked on me. Once a week, I knew I could talk about the emotional vortex I felt. And just talking about it helped, I came to realize. Without the group, when would I have the chance to let out even a little of the pent-up anguish? *With* the group, we vented a little bit each week. Marilene and I left the session each week with the sense that a tiny bit of the burden might have lifted. Plus we felt that our participation helped others, which was also rewarding.

After a few months with the group, which had helped us hugely, a couple of patterns emerged. We noticed that certain people played a tape loop. You would hear their wrenching story in January. Then seven or eight meetings later, in March, you would hear the same story. As I've noted elsewhere, there is no one "right" way to manage grief; we all must handle it as best we individually can handle it. For some, I imagine that they need to circle a track many times—maybe even for years—before they can find an off-ramp, a fresh start, a new chapter.

A second pattern or dynamic that emerged with the group was the different experiences with the spiritual aspect of what we were going through. By this I do not mean the religious aspect. Religion popped up on any number of occasions, but never in any kind of proselytizing way. Religion came up incidentally, in connection with burial customs or memorial services.

No, when I bring up differential experiences with the spiritual, I refer to people's encounters with their passed loved ones, whether in the form of signs or messages, or even more-direct manifestations. After several months in the group, we saw that maybe a third of the group had had experiences that they attributed to their passed son or daughter. So that meant that two-thirds had not shared such experiences. Furthermore, neither of our two facilitators had had any impactful experiences of their passed sons. In fact, once or twice I thought I sensed a little irritation on the part of one or the other facilitator if Marilene or I shared one of our Kevin anecdotes. No one ever discouraged us overtly, but I found myself wondering if they became agitated that someone (us) might be dangling false hope or flirting with the envelope of the permissible from a beliefs standpoint. Or they may have been nervous about cliques forming, some people feeling deprived.

Whatever the underlying driver, Marilene and I began to feel a slight tension in the group. As much as the group had helped us, and as much as we cared about the others in the group, we began to drift, to feel pulled in another direction. We will be forever grateful for the grief support group and would recommend it highly to any parent in the same unfortunate position. But for us, it is a chapter that we finally wound down.

This Is Where You Can Reach Me Now

On March 16, 2019, Marilene took a break from tidying the house to retrieve her smartphone. When she did, something odd stared up at her from the screen. Two unsent text messages—both written to her sister Maristela—sat in the blue text-bubbles. Both were the same exact message, but neither sent.

The messages said: "I am listening to 'This is Where You Can Reach Me Now' by U2."

Marilene has no explanation for how these notes got there; *she* didn't type them. She went ahead and sent one to Maristela, followed quickly with another note to Maristela explaining that she hadn't written the message. They spoke on the phone and marveled at it.

Of course, as soon as I heard about this, we needed to pull up that song. I sprinted to my Spotify account and pulled it up.

As with many U2 songs, this one tugged at that part of you that longs for something or someone. It begins with what sounds like a tribal drum. A two-note, high-low piano couplet joins, then climbs a stairstep of notes, followed by a lead guitar twanging a forlorn, brooding refrain. Finally a wailing synthesizer track feeds in, threading through it all with a sustained, foreign lilt.

We had to listen to it a few times to capture all the lyrics. As we "got" more and more of the lyrics, Marilene and I stared at each other, mouths slowly opening in amazement, and knowing.

This could only have come from Kevin.

I cannot reproduce the lyrics verbatim here, but the song struck the tuning fork for us in a number of ways. Bono sings to an unknown soldier, as if he (Bono) too, is a soldier. He goes on so say that they sign their lives away. But the next paradox in the song is that complete surrender is the only weapon they know. In another stanza, Bono refers to an old man who knows that he (Bono) never listens. Later, he begins a new stanza saying that they (he and whoever he's with, presumably) come from an ancient place. And finally, of course, the song wraps with "This Is Where You Can Reach Me Now."

Kevin was nothing if not a soldier in his battle with cancer. I have referred elsewhere to how stubborn he could be, and how he often refused to listen to me or Marilene. At the end, of course, all that was left to Kevin was complete surrender. And the haunting conclusion of where we can reach him now sealed it for us.

The song ran to Kevin's tastes. He had a lot of U2 on his playlists. It is very well produced, the musical tracks ones you want to hear in surround-sound to achieve the full immersion experience. It evokes a mood, compels you to listen, and draws you in. You begin to wonder: *From where is he singing? From what source or context came these words? And how does his world interplay with mine?*

A New Path Opening

After our October 2018 experience with the psychic medium Bill Philipps in San Francisco, we got excited when we saw that he would be doing a workshop in Santa Cruz in March 2019. We bought tickets and arranged accommodations right away.

It turned out that the venue for this workshop was a place in the Santa Cruz mountains called 1440 Multiversity. This triggered an interesting coincidence: 1440 is owned by the cousin of our good friend Marci Kriens. Marci had been prodding us to go to 1440 for a couple years. So she agreed to join us for Philipps workshop, called "Divine Wisdom."

"Divine Wisdom" was programmed to run for a couple hours Friday evening, a full day Saturday, and until mid-day on Sunday. I felt that the name of the workshop perhaps didn't exactly resonate with the content. Quite different from the show we had attended at the comedy club the prior October in San Francisco, this workshop was designed to awaken and stimulate the latent medium capabilities in us, the workshop participants.

Now, whatever layers of skepticism I may have sheathed myself in say, a year before, much had been stripped away at Philipps's October show. And not only that, but in the months since he had passed, I had felt and sensed Kevin, had observed unmistakable signs that he was still around us, and that he watched over us and even responded to requests. So I went to "Divine Wisdom" with Marilene with a welcoming and open mind.

The 1440 Multiversity is a beautiful campus and lodge in the Santa Cruz mountains, on eighty acres of ridges, redwoods, and streams. The multiversity embraces advanced learning in curricula ranging from health and well-being to meditation and mindfulness, and of course to the spiritual. The "Divine Wisdom" course took place in a spacious auditorium near the center of the campus. On the first evening, the class participants assembled for the session. Of two dozen participants, most of us were in our forties or older. We arranged our folding chairs in a semi-circle in front of a low stage at the front of the auditorium. I noticed I was one of three men.

The fact that women outnumbered men wasn't a big surprise. Men seem to seldom reveal that they're open to the spiritual world, at least in my experience, and not often around other men.

But that ratio—21 to 3—surprised me a bit. It could have been stifling or intimidating for me, but I saw it instead this way: if women are more open to the spiritual, then they would make better conduits, better classmates, and maybe some of their ability would somehow rub off. Anyway, I looked forward to the program.

Bill—I'll call him that from now on—started us off slowly. He explained first what would be taking place over the three days. Then he took us through a meditation for about twenty minutes. This meditation was designed to open us up, to energize our chakras, and to protect us in divine white light.

Next Bill had us attempt a simple exercise in psychometry. You might think of ESP (extrasensory perception) cards. We broke into pairs. The goal of the exercise was to try to sense what was on the card based only on what your partner could see. The partner would look at the card, then tuck it into an envelope. I approached this exercise with an open mind, but low expectations. When I touched one envelope containing a card, and rubbed it on my forehead, an image popped into my mind. The image was of a light-colored or white figure, with what looked like outstretched wings. I actually demonstrated to my partner by extending my own arms out to either side. Upon opening the envelope, the image on the card had a light-colored background. In the foreground, two dark "cliffs" leaned-in over a gorge, facing each other, the gap between them narrowing until at the top the cliff rims were quite close. Then, stretched between the rims of the two cliffs was the figure of a man, his feet at one rim and his hands clutching the rim of the other. The effect of the light background, fronted by the two dark wedge-like cut-outs (the cliffs), closely resembled the shape of the image that had popped into my mind. And the figure of the man with outstretched arms, straddling the two cliff-rims, almost echoed my own pantomime with my partner.

I was kind of tickled—coming with no expectations—that I had sensed something which conformed as closely as it did with the image on the card. Some of the other participants got even closer than I did. Marilene sensed a big white mustache. When she flipped the card, it carried an image of an old man with a white flowing beard and mustache! Marci "saw" a clown. Sure enough, there was a clown on her card! For the class as a whole, the "hit-rate" of correct or near-correct reads vastly exceeded what anyone could have expected by pure chance, especially since the majority of us were—like Marilene, Marci, and me—rank rookies.

But we were done for the evening. What was to come the next day would make the psychometry exercise look like child's play.

We started Day 2 as we had Day 1: with meditation to open us up and protect us. Next, we did an interesting exercise "reading" photos of people, trying to suss out their personalities. A few people in the class correctly sensed that one sunny-looking woman in a photo had actually killed her children. Others intuited, also correctly, that a somber-looking, Nordic man in another photo had been persecuted by the Nazis in WWII.

Bill then took us through another meditation, designed for us to encounter our spirit guide. In his calm, soothing voice, Bill first took us to a beautiful beach, on our way to a cave lit from within, where we would encounter our guide. But, while I was still "on the beach," small waves gently lapping on the shore, Kevin popped into view on my right. He was healthy, full head of hair, wearing all white: white pants, rolled up to mid-shin for the beach, and a white long-sleeved shirt, cuffs rolled up to the elbows. He was jogging up the beach, to my right, looking back at me over his left shoulder, smiling. In mid-stride he leapt, saying, "Look, Dad! I'm fine!" And he leapt again, playfully, still looking at me with a smile. I said, "Oh, son, is this really you?!"

We walked up the beach together. At this point, tears were streaming down the face of the me in the auditorium, and I didn't try to wipe them; I was afraid I'd lose this…whatever this was.

Kevin didn't seem to "follow" me as we went into the cave in the meditation. I tried to follow Bill's guidance for the rest of the exercise, but I don't think I was effective, after the beach.

Now, someone reading this could reasonably ask, "Well, was this Kevin? Or was this you wishing for or conjuring Kevin, placing him into the scene in your meditation?" I agree. I had the same question. As a rookie to all of this, I felt unable to tell the difference between me wanting to see Kevin, and "placing" him in the scene in the meditation, versus Kevin entering the scene. So I asked Bill about it.

Bill's response to the question was immediate: "How did you *feel* when it happened?" He went on. "If it just appeared as an image, like a photo, without feeling, then it was you. If you had strong feelings when it happened, then it was Kevin."

Could it be that straightforward? I thought. Of course, this wasn't proof positive. But we weren't dealing with the scientific method here, were we? We knew we had been in touch with Kevin the prior October because the weight of proof-points had been overwhelming. But on reflection, all those proof-points were rooted in deep feelings. We knew and accepted that Kevin was reaching out to us, offering signs that he was with us, still. If I accepted *that,* and I did, was it really a leap now to accept what Bill had just told me, especially given how strongly, how involuntarily, the feelings had come? I had wept profusely when I saw Kevin. The feeling was powerful.

A little later on Day 2, Bill moved us through another meditation. This time, we walked near a waterfall next to a pond. Around to the side of the pond, we saw a glass elevator, brightly lit. Bill guided us toward the elevator.

As I "walked" toward the elevator, Kevin again appeared, this time waiting for me in the elevator. He wore the same white clothes, was barefoot and smiling. I entered the elevator, went to him, and without stopping gave him the biggest bear-hug I could, lasting for several long seconds. This time, tears streamed down my face *both* in the meditation and in the auditorium. I thought I might burst from happiness. Bill was trying to guide us through a meditation where the elevator rose us to a higher consciousness, but I just wanted to stay with Kevin. I do not now remember the rest of that meditation.

Later on in Day 2, Bill moved us on to a new exercise. We paired up again, with different people this time. I ended up with a nice woman named Clare.

Bill assigned an exercise to write a question we wanted an answer to on a sheet of paper, which we then placed into an envelope. We would hand the envelope to our partner, then hold hands, seated across from each other, close our eyes, and try to discern the answer to our partner's question.

When I closed my eyes and tried to open myself to receive the answer to Clare's question, the first thing that entered my mind was "Make sure the roles are clear," which I shared with Clare. I shared one other piece of counsel, which I cannot now remember.

The next moment—still with my eyes shut—the phrase "*Carpe Diem*.... Seize the Day!" entered my mind. I shared this with Clare. Then I returned to concentrating, sure I could get more.

To my surprise, Clare cut me off, and released my hands from hers. She said, "Stop. You've said enough already."

I opened my eyes, unsure if I'd offended, somehow. Clare was crying. I was a little alarmed, but at the same time I had to know: What nerve had I touched? What had I received that so moved her?

Clare explained. "The question I was trying to answer was: 'Should I pursue a collaboration that's been offered to me?" she began. "My husband, a surgeon with a well-known reputation, passed away eighteen months ago from cancer. Recently, I've been offered a chance to collaborate on a book about what we can learn from a cancer experience."

I gazed at Clare, in sympathy for her loss, but still puzzled about why she had cut off my "reading."

She continued. "My husband—on a Friday night or a weekend morning—used to say, 'Let's go do something. *Carpe Diem!*' He said it all the time."

My eyes popped to full-open; my jaw dropped and hung there. "Are you *kidding* me?" I finally got out.

Smiling but still sniffling, Clare hugged me. She said, "Thank you. You've really got something, you know it?"

But whatever I had, I was a novice at this. Our group had some serious connections with the other side, as I was about to hear.

Just as I was pairing with Clare for this exercise, Marilene had crossed the room seeking her next partner. She was at the point of agreeing to pair with someone, when a woman came up from behind her and said, "You wanna partner?" This was more statement than request. The woman turned to head back to her chair.

Marilene said, "S-s-sure" and followed her.

The two staged their chairs facing each other. Marilene's partner turned out to be a woman named Jamie. They held hands.

Within a minute or two, Jamie became visibly agitated. She kept holding Marilene's hands, but she started sobbing. "So much pain. So much love. I can't take it." She opened her eyes. "I have to hug you." They hugged. She continued to cry. Marilene was stunned. It wasn't clear if Jamie would be able to continue.

All of this did not escape the notice of Bill Philipps. He came over, soothed Jamie. "It's okay. It's okay. Take some deep breaths." He rejoined their hands together. "Breathe. Let it come to you."

Jamie resumed, somewhat more collected now. She spoke to Marilene. "I see the image of a young man. He's behind you. He's hugging you from behind. He's got his head on your shoulder."

Note: Several months before he passed, Marilene told me of something that had happened that day. She had been at the stove, cooking something, when Kevin came up from behind her, wrapped both arms around her, placed his head on her shoulder, and saying lovingly, "Mamae" (Portuguese for Mama). Kevin was not often demonstrative or affectionate in this way; it had made her day, and she said so.

Jamie went on to describe a little dog! Black, brown highlights, white socks. She said it was playing with the young man. Chloe, playing with Kevin; there could be no doubt. And it echoed what Bill Philipps had said in the club in San Francisco some five months before. When Marilene and Jamie broke, hugging each other once more, Marilene sought me out and told me the story.

We reflected on it later. The insistent way in which Jamie approached Marilene about teaming up with her, coupled with what had happened in her reading with Marilene, had all the earmarks of coming from something more than Jamie.

But this anecdote has legs. At the dining lodge that evening, Jamie and her mother swung by where we ate, and handed Marilene a wrapped package. "I was told to buy this for you," Jamie said. Marilene, obviously intrigued, looked up at Jamie, then over to me, before untying the ribbon and tearing open the paper.

Inside the package was a set of windchimes. *Dragonfly* windchimes. Jamie continued, "I had stopped by the gift shop. Kevin told me to get this for you." She paused. "Kevin hasn't left me alone. He said he really wanted to thank me for connecting you today."

We could not find the words. Now in full transparency, Marilene and I had mentioned dragonflies once in passing, earlier in the workshop. But Jamie's/Kevin's gesture was so touching and so *personal* that we got goosebumps.

At breakfast the next day, Jamie again found Marilene. "Does Kevin like to joke around?"

Marilene admitted that yeah, that sounded like Kevin. He loved to tell jokes and play pranks on people.

Jamie went on. "He wouldn't leave me alone last night. Kept telling me jokes until 2 a.m."

Marilene and I laughed. But we told Jamie she had to lay down the law with Kevin if he was getting in the way of her sleep! She had our permission to tell him to knock it off. But once more, later—on reflection—Kevin's manner with Jamie echoed exactly the way he had imposed himself on Dylan at first, until they became great friends. And as before, at Bill's October show in San Francisco, we came away dumbstruck at not only *what* we had received at Multiversity, but also *how* it came across. In every respect, it said Kevin.

Whatever nascent abilities Marilene or I awakened at the "Divine Wisdom" program, Jamie and a few others showed us that there are people around us who can tune in to a reality several layers beyond the common.

Asks

Marilene was having a bad day. I could hear her crying in the shower, as I stretched out on the bed. It was about 1 a.m. I shut off the lamp on the nightstand, but the light on Marilene's nightstand remained on.

As I lay there, not yet sleepy, I got the distinct feeling that Kevin was right there, to my right, next to the bed. It wasn't that I could see him or hear anything. The only way I can explain it is that I felt his presence, a subtle but certain shift in the vibration in the air, almost like that charge in the air during a thunderstorm just before lightning strikes, and a familiar vibe that made me think of Kevin. When I felt that he was there, of course I perked up, heightening my senses, trying to dial it in better. This was in no way scary. In fact, it was easy, warm, loving, and somehow…I felt that Kevin was…available.

And so I spoke to him. "Hey, son. I love you, buddy. You know, your mom is having a tough day; she misses you so much. We both do, of course. But if there's some sign you can give her—some comfort—well, it would mean a lot to her."

A minute or so later, Marilene emerged from her shower, put on her pajamas, and sniffling a bit, still, sat on the edge of the bed. Her phone chimed. A message came in from Brazil on WhatsApp. She picked up her phone and opened the message.

The message was from her sister Marina in Paraguassu. At this time, Brazil was about six hours ahead of us, so it would have been 7 a.m. or so there. Marina shared an interesting little story. Her daughter Renata told Marina of a dream she had just had. In the dream, Renata received a present for *her* daughter. Renata was six months pregnant at this time; her daughter was not yet born. But the gift was a little set of denim overalls. The note which accompanied the overalls said "With deepest love and warmth, your cousin Kevin" (in Portuguese, of course). Renata was so moved by the dream, and it had been so clear and vivid, that she had called her mother right away upon waking, to tell her about it. And Marina relayed the story immediately to Marilene.

Marilene cried more then, but now it was out of joy and gratitude. I told her about feeling Kevin in the room, and the ask I had made of him.

Start to finish, this whole episode transpired over four or five minutes.

We often relax in the evening with a glass of wine and a movie on Netflix or some other subscription service. A broad spectrum of movies appeals to me. I can watch drama, historical period pieces, horror, sci-fi, crime stories, supernatural, documentaries, sports-themed, fantasy, you name it. Marilene's tastes run, shall we say, to a much narrower slice of the movie universe. So the biggest ordeal is selecting a movie on which we can both agree. I do not exaggerate when I say that it can often take 30-40 minutes to agree on a film. The movie-selection process gets so tiring that honestly, sometimes I think I should go watch something upstairs while she chooses something in the family room.

One evening I waited on the sofa while Marilene showered. When she came downstairs in her pajamas and bathrobe and declared herself movie-ready, I picked up the remote and settled in for the move-selection marathon. Here we go.

As soon as I called up the assortment of available films, the third option was a new (to us) film. This film had not been on the menu before that day. And we knew this because we accessed this movie list at least five times a week. The film that caught our eye was called *The Sea of Trees.* The description of the movie said "A stranger takes a troubled teacher on a life-changing journey through Japan's Aokigahara forest." The film starred Matthew McConaughey, Naomi Watts, and Ken Watanabe, and was directed by Gus Van Sant. We liked those actors and that director, so we agreed to watch this one. We marveled at how quickly we chose; we had never agreed so quickly on a film before.

As the story unfolds, we learn that Matthew McConaughey plays a teacher who has lost his wife (Naomi Watts). He had cared for her through a critical illness before she died. He is so distraught that he travels to Japan, to the Aokigahara Forest near Mount Fuji. This forest is famously haunted by the tortured souls of all the people who go there to commit suicide. This actual forest covers thousands of acres near the slopes of Mount Fuji. One can easily get lost there. McConaughey's character intends to end his life there.

McConaughey hikes into the forest, disregarding the signs (in Japanese, with English sub-script) asking hikers not to leave the marked paths, seeking a spot to swallow an overdose of pills. As the film takes us and McConaughey deeper and deeper into the forest, we get a panorama of nature played out over a brooding undercurrent. Under the thick canopy of green, McConaughey passes by evidence of others: discarded ID's, backpacks, scraps of clothing, even a skeleton. The camera lingers on a close-up of a magnificent dragonfly with red markings; it fills the entire screen.

Marilene and I hiked an eyebrow at each other. Dragonflies have taken on major significance for us since Kevin passed. In fact, we believe that he sends them to get our attention. But this was one brief scene; we said nothing and just kept watching the movie.

McConaughey finds a high spot, seated on a rock, which appears to suit his mission. He sits cross-legged, reaches into the inside pocket of his trench coat, and extracts an envelope, which he sets beside him on the rock. A close-up of the envelope shows that it is addressed to his dead wife. That address is in Natick, Massachusetts.

Another hiked eyebrow, eyes widened this time. We lived in Natick between '03 and '06.

McConaughey takes out of another pocket a bottle of pills. He takes one pill with water from a bottle he brought; then another. But just then, he spots a figure through the trees, staggering, before falling to its knees. McConaughey hesitates but decides to go see to the stranger. He walks over to the stranger, a Japanese man (Ken Watanabe), and helps him to his feet. We learn that he came here to die but reconsidered and now wants to return home to his family. Watanabe implores McConaughey for help to get him back to the parking lot at the trailhead. McConaughey at first tries to separate from Watanabe, directing him back to the trail. But Watanabe has been in the forest two days. He has cuts on his wrists, and he is very weakened. McConaughey realizes that Watanabe will not make it out on his own, so he suspends his suicide plans, for the moment, to help him.

Between segments of the film taking place in the Japanese forest, we get flashbacks to McConaughey's life with his wife. During one flashback, while she's at the hospital, a doctor mentions that they plan to transfer the wife to another facility called St. Mary's.

Before he died, Kevin completed his freshman year at St. Mary's College.

Back in the forest, over two days and nights, through exertion and mishaps, Watanabe's condition worsens. McConaughey realizes finally that Watanabe is too injured and weakened, he is slowing them up, and he (McConaughey) must go for help to have any hope of saving him. He helps Watanabe take shelter in an abandoned tent, assures him that he'll return, tells him to hang on, and prepares to set off. Before he does, Watanabe grabs his arm and says, "Thank you for taking care of me."

McConaughey hikes out, finally finds help in the form of some forest rangers, and asks them to return to the forest to find and help Watanabe. The rangers scour the forest across several square miles, find a tent that matches the description that McConaughey gave them, but no Watanabe and no sign that he was there and left. They can find no family with the name that McConaughey gave them, either.

After a hospital stay in Japan, and some counseling, McConaughey returns to the States. Near the film's end, he opens the envelope that he had in the forest, the one addressed to his wife. She had ordered a copy of her favorite children's book. In the envelope is a copy of an old edition of *Hansel and Gretel*.

When he was five, we took Kevin to a theatrical performance of *Hansel and Gretel* at the famous Teatro Colon in Buenos Aires, when we lived there. We even kept a program from that performance in our coffee table for twelve years.

In *The Sea of Trees* there's a twist at the end of the film, which I don't want to spoil. But by the end, the McConaughey character receives a message from his passed wife in a way that's inescapable.

Only after the movie did Marilene tell me that she had been crying in the shower. This happens regularly, even now. But she went on to say that she had asked Kevin for a sign, something that said he was okay.

So, to recap, Marilene pleads with Kevin for a sign. Immediately there-after, we spot a movie in the listing which had not been there even the day before. We agreed to that movie in seconds, when for us, normally getting to agreement on a movie is nearly impossible. The film features an accumulation of references that strike a note between us and Kevin: the dragonfly with the red highlights; Natick, MA; "Thank you for tak-ing care of me"; St. Mary's; *Hansel and Gretel.* And—to tie a ribbon on it—the film is about a man who sees a loved one through a critical illness, she dies, he becomes distraught and desperate, and at the end he gets an unambiguous loving message from his passed loved one. The film works as presented. It is heartfelt and mystical, the performances come off as authentic, and the main character restarts his life when he knows that his wife still loves him from beyond.

There we sat—one layer or concentric circle further out from the story—its messages and references so relevant and so personal it felt as if it had been written for us and shared just at the moment we needed it.

Game, set, match. And with more elegance and style than I knew he possessed. Thank you, son. That meant a lot to your mom that day; to both of us.

Did I mention that the film was made in 2015…?

Blake

One of Kevin's best friends, Blake O'Brien, had his twentieth birthday in March 2019. Blake goes to Washington State University. Waking up on his birthday, he felt and missed Kevin. He realized that this was his first birthday without Kevin, and it made him a bit low, a bit thoughtful.

As he got ready to go about his day, Blake said, "Kev, I miss ya, partner. If you're okay, I would consider it a great birthday gift if you could give me some kind of sign. Love ya, man." He went about his day, which unfolded fairly routinely.

That evening, Blake and his girlfriend Izzy and two friends relaxed on the sofa in his room.

Suddenly they heard a thud in his closet. Blake got up to see what the noise was. He inspected his closet but didn't find anything obviously out of place, except a shoebox standing up on its end, as opposed to its bottom. In his mind, he addressed Kevin. "Hey, Kev. I *think* you just gave me a sign, but so that I'm sure, can you send me an insurance sign?"

Not long after that, a water bottle which had stood drying near the kitchen sink for a day and a half toppled over. Blake told me that there is no window near that countertop, nor any vents which could have sent a stream of air in that direction.

The next morning, Blake was getting ready to go out. He stood before his dresser, chatting with Izzy, who sat on the bed behind him. As Blake reached for his smartphone on one side of the dresser, he stopped in midsentence. He felt a warm rush come over him, and he felt as if Kevin was with him. At that exact moment, a tissue poking up out of a Kleenex box on the other side of the dresser began to flutter and kept doing so for several seconds. Once more, no windows were open in that room, nor was the box positioned near any vents.

Blake said it was the best birthday gift he received.

Easter 2019

Our journey with spirit continues. Today—April 21, 2019—is Easter Sunday. After an Easter brunch, Marilene and I decided to take a hike in nearby Port Costa, followed by some refreshment. The only place open in Port Costa this Easter Sunday was The Warehouse, a pub-bar-café. The building was used a hundred years ago for wheat storage.

The Warehouse didn't have many customers this afternoon. We walked in, strode over to the bar, and took up a couple barstools next to a couple nursing their drinks. The bartender delivered our beers, and the man seated next to us engaged us.

"Happy Easter," the man offered, in a friendly way. I gauged him to be mid-sixties, nearly bald, fairly heavy-set. He wore glasses, the kind without frames around the lenses. On the bar in front of him sat a greenish cocktail and the remains of a pinkish one. Beside him, and partly screened from our vision, sat a woman I assumed was his wife. She had dark hair, looked Latin, and at first glance she appeared to listen but not engage us with eye contact, seeming to prefer the company of her Corona.

"And to you!" I replied, raising my glass. Marilene mimicked me.

The heavy, bald man began to chat. *Uh-oh*, I thought. *Motor-mouth alert*. To myself, I predicted a one-beer stay and a hasty escape.

Three hours—and an equal number of beers each—later, Marilene and I walked out of the Warehouse in a semi-daze. The daze was not beer-driven. It was because freaky things keep happening to us.

We learned that our bar companions were named Kenneth and Alicia. Alicia was from Puerto Vallarta. They had been married sixteen years. They lived in an unincorporated zone between the cities of El Cerrito and

Richmond. Over the course of those three hours, we unraveled one co-incidence after another with this couple we met on "chance encounter."

Kenneth and Alicia are nine years apart in age. Marilene and I are nine years apart in age.

Alicia is Latina, from Mexico. Of course, Marilene is Latina, from Brazil.

Kenneth and Alicia's house is about six blocks from the house I lived in growing up from 1971 to 1984.

Kenneth and I both went to the same high school: Kennedy High in Richmond. He graduated in 1971. I graduated in 1974. We each named teachers there.

Kenneth's grandfather was Norwegian. Mine was Danish. Kenneth's grandfather built the house Kenneth lives in and has lived in for sixty-three years.

Kenneth and Alicia have a Chihuahua named Chloe. Of course, we had a mutt rat terrier named Chloe, until November of 2018, when we had to put her to sleep. Now Chloe is a fairly common name for a dog, but I wasn't ready for the next thing. Growing up, Kenneth had a dog named Thunder's Thor. When I was growing up, we had a mutt black Labrador named Thor! Both Thors lived to the ripe old age of seventeen!

But all these coincidences were placed there in order to get our atten-tion. The *story* that Kenneth (the first two letters of his name were not lost on me, either) and Alicia told was what we were supposed to hear and internalize. The coincidences were simply teasers: *Hello? Paying attention yet?!*

Because the story of Kenneth and Alicia so closely mirrored our own, and Kevin's.

Kenneth and Alicia met when they both worked at an Orchard Supply Hardware store. Kenneth was trying to chat up Alicia. But at first she was having none of it (*another* parallel, similar to how Marilene rebuffed me when I first tried to chat her up!). Alicia was a single mom, raising two kids. But Alicia was in severe pain. She had almost incapacitating pain in her abdomen.

Kenneth asked her about it. "Why don't you go to the doctor?"

She replied, "I can't afford it."

On his lunch break that same day, Kenneth went home and to the ATM and pulled out what cash he could muster, stuffed it into an envelope, and brought it to Alicia that afternoon.

"What's this?" Alicia asked.

"It's for you, to go to the doctor," Kenneth said.

"But I can't repay you," Alicia complained.

"Don't worry about that. You need to go to the doctor," Kenneth insisted.

Once Alicia had been to a proper doctor, she was diagnosed with fibroids. This is a type of tumor that had to be removed surgically. It was found to be benign, but even so it came back, and several months later she needed a complete hysterectomy. Since then, she has been fine.

As the conversation unfolded, and one bizarre coincidence after another clicked into place, I abandoned the one-beer plan. Our bartender Nancy had a loud but charismatic personality. In between f-bombs and opening my next hefeweizen, she dropped that she was a Cal Bears fan. That's where I went to school.

After two beers, I needed to hit the men's room. I learned later what happened while I was away.

While I was in the men's room, Kenneth and Alicia asked Marilene if we had any kids. Marilene handled this in the way we often do. She said, "We have two boys," hoping that that would tie off that line of questioning. But

Alicia pressed. Where do they go to school? Marilene offered, "Our oldest went to St. Mary's College. Our younger one goes to Boston University."

It turned out that one of Alicia's sons (from her first marriage) also went to St. Mary's. Granted, St. Mary's is a college quite close to where both we and Kenneth and Alicia live. But if you pile enough coincidences on that side of the scale, even the most stubborn skeptic must at some point cry "Uncle."

But Alicia persisted. "Oh, what's your older boy studying at St. Mary's?" Finally, Marilene admitted that we had lost Kevin last year. When I returned from the men's room, Marilene was showing Alicia pictures of both boys.

As our conversation ripened, Kenneth shared that he was diabetic, suffered from arthritis, and wasn't moving around that well any more. He implied that Alicia had saved his life more than once. He had taken care of Alicia before they got married, and they would take care of each other going forward. He even got emotional a couple of times, and apologized, where none was necessary.

As we finished our last beers, Kenneth delivered a fitting summation of our wonderful conversation. "You know, you can meet a lot of people who seem friendly or engaging at first. But the ones that matter," and he motioned to his wife, then to Marilene, "are the ones who support you and take care of you in the hard times. We need to support and take care of each other."

Marilene and I said warm thanks and goodbyes to Kenneth and Alicia, departed the Warehouse, and got back in the car for the ride home. We spoke little, spending chunks of time deep in thought about what had just happened.

At some point, you just have to stop talking yourself out of what's happening. What's happening is that you're receiving messages, and you would have to be willfully ignorant not to pay attention. In fact, it got so that I thought it would be actually *disrespectful* to not pay attention.

April 23, 2019

Claire and Hannah came over for dinner tonight. Claire is the girl that Kevin fell in love with the first several weeks at St. Mary's, but who had a boyfriend. Hannah became a close friend of Kevin's. They are approaching their final exams of their sophomore years at St. Mary's, and it was a Tuesday, so it was kind of them to take time on a "school night" to come over. But, as Claire said, "I'll *make* the time for a home-cooked meal!"

The evening was warm, so we settled in with cold beers and chardonnays. And we talked. We talked a lot about Kevin.

"Kevin just seemed to *know* everybody." Hannah said. "We'd be cruising the halls, and Kevin would acknowledge several people as we passed. He'd introduce us to these other guys he knew. We were so new and unsure of ourselves then, it was like a welcome mat for us. We latched on to Kevin right away."

"I met Kevin almost the first day of school," Claire said. She looked off somewhere toward the back of the kitchen. "I'll tell ya what: he got me through that English class, with Professor Cooney. That one was going to be tough, if I hadn't met Kevin." She went on to tell me about one day in that English class. "After class, Kevin and I usually walked together. But one day, Kevin asked me to hold up. He said, 'I need to check on Cooney. Did you notice he was in pain?' I replied, 'No, I hadn't.' But Kevin was right. Cooney was battling sciatica, during and through the class. And Kevin noticed it."

I had heard of this same anecdote through another lens: that of Professor Cooney himself. "I suffer from chronic pain, due to sciatica," he told me one day. "During one class early in the semester, it was pretty bad. I am accustomed to masking it and getting on with the task at hand. And usually, I think no one else notices what's going on. But this one day, right after I wrapped up class, Kevin caught me at my office. 'Hey, are you okay?' he asked me. This surprised me slightly, as I didn't think I had telegraphed that I was in discomfort during the class. 'I know something about pain,' Kevin offered. And it was only then that I learned what Kevin had gone through in his first two battles with cancer. What so impressed me about it was how empathetic and sensitive he was. That's rare with kids this age."

We asked Claire and Hannah about the day that Kevin told them about his cancer returning. His mates at St. Mary's knew that Kevin had had it twice before.

"What struck me so much," Claire began, "was how composed he was. He wasn't emotional or upset, as I would be, or as I think most people would be."

Hannah chimed in. "It was almost as if he was trying to console *us*," she began. "He stayed upbeat, no matter what was going on with him, even months later, when it was getting pretty bad."

Claire caught us up on news in her life. "I broke up with my boyfriend," she shared. "It was just too much. He was jealous, kinda controlling. He would get jealous of Kevin, of Dylan."

Claire continued. "Funny thing: after I broke up with him, I walked out to my car, got in, shut the door. I just sat there for a minute." She paused a moment, looking off, remembering. "Just then, a dragonfly flew right up to my windshield, on the driver's side, just inches from the window, and hovered there several seconds, as if looking right at me. Then it flew off." Another brief pause. "I sat there for several minutes more."

After another pause, where we all sipped our drinks, she continued. "Kevin told me how he felt." I was happy to hear her say this. Kevin admitted to me how he felt about Claire, and during one of our long stays at UCSF I told him I thought he should let her know. "And I felt the same toward him, but I was involved with somebody else at the time.

"Kevin changed me. Permanently. Before, I think I 'made do' with guys that were not good for me. Now, I measure any new guys I meet against that standard, the Kevin standard. And that's a pretty high bar, but I don't care, because I would rather be single than 'make do' again."

"I think Kevin will find a way to let you know how he feels about the next guy," I grinned.

Bat

One evening in September 2019, something outside the view window overlooking our deck caught my peripheral vision. I cocked my head over in that direction. It was dusk. The sun had set, but the sky over the horizon was still pale-light.

A bat wheeled and circled around the oak which grows through the hole in the center of our deck. We had lived in this house for almost a year and a half; this was the first time I had seen a bat.

I watched the creature for three or four minutes. It wheeled and dipped and whipped this way and that, circling the oak the whole time. Of course, I have seen a number of bats in my lifetime, flitting and diving, seeking whatever insect prey that I could not see. Their maneuverability and stamina always impressed me. They're quite entertaining to watch.

But our bat on that September evening flew with abandon, with zeal, with *joy.* Joy was the word that popped into my mind as I watched its display. *Look at meeeeeee! Look what I can dooooooo!*

Four days after that, Marilene had a phone reading with a medium in England. No, we do not seek sessions with every medium who crosses our radar. But in this case, a friend we trust had referred us, and Marilene took a stab. She had had this phone appointment set up a week or so before.

Several things this medium shared resonated strongly with Kevin. By this time, we were convinced enough of the legitimacy of the practice of mediumship that we were not often bowled over by things. Some mediums were less impressive, to be sure. And we would not return to those. But others shared things that felt like a jolt from a light socket. At one point in this reading, the English medium said to Marilene, "I'm getting a bat, or bats. Have you seen any bats lately?" Marilene admitted that yes, we had just seen one a few nights before, for the first time since we had been in this house. "That's him, Kevin says," shared the medium. "He says he sent the bat as a message."

"I'm Okay."

Only several months after Kevin's service did we hear the following story.

Our good friend Katrina O'Brien, over a glass of wine, mentioned that her husband Paul is a "sensitive," meaning he senses people who've passed. He's had this almost his whole life. Katrina went on to say that Paul had heard from Kevin during the service at St. Mary's.

Two sets of eyes opened wide! Marilene and I pressed Katrina: What did Kevin say? Katrina shared some generalities but said it might be best to ask Paul himself about it.

So we had to sit in aching suspense, but an opportunity presented itself a few weeks later, when the O'Briens invited us over for dinner. We settled in, snacking on chips and sipping some wine. At an opportune moment, when only Marilene, Paul, and I were in the kitchen, I kind of cornered Paul.

"Paul, I hope I'm not putting you too much on the spot, but Katrina shared that you heard from Kevin during the service, is that right?" I asked. "Marilene and I are dying to know what you heard. You think you are able to share it?"

Paul—a tall, rugged fireman by profession—teared up immediately. "Sorry, I don't do too well with this stuff." But he took a deep breath, somewhat composed himself, and shared. "I heard his voice. He said 'Mr. O'Brien, why is everybody so sad? Please tell them I'm fine!'"

Paul went on to share a couple other stories from his past—non-Kevin ones—relating to this unwanted ability he has. It's been with him almost his whole life; he recounted a couple other compelling anecdotes.

What Paul had shared fit in to a larger picture whose pieces we received over several months and continue to receive today. Kevin wants us to know that he is well, happy, and active—even watching over us—and sending regular messages.

Grant

Grant Pisenti became one of Kevin's very best friends, especially their junior and senior years at San Ramon Valley High. They played on the football team together, hung out together, and made each other better. The following are excerpts from a chat that Grant and I had on April 16, 2019, when he was at college in Colorado.

Kevin vibrated with such positivity all the time, no matter what he was going through. He was always about "Do the things that make you happy."

Kevin and I had this thing where we called each other "Lord." So he was "Lord Kevin," and I was "Lord Grant." For a while Zach was "Squire Zach." It all started as a joke. "Squire" didn't stick, but somehow, "Lord" did stick. After Kevin passed, it took on more meaning.

For a while, early in high school, I was struggling socially. I was really shy, unsure. But Kevin, Zach, and Spencer—and especially Kevin— opened me up. Kevin showed me how to be happy, goofy sometimes. And I carry that with me now, and I'm happier for it.

Early this semester, I was living in a house with four friends. I took an Accounting exam and thought I had screwed it up; thought I may have earned a C or even a D. Also, at that same time, some of my roommates were failing on the cleaning front, and I was picking up the slack. The cleanliness thing got bad enough that I thought I would need to change my living situation, and I felt it was affecting me academically.

So, feeling like I needed some guidance, I asked Kevin for a favor. I asked him what I should do next, how I should resolve my living situation, and what I should do academically and for my major.

Over the following week, I learned that I actually got an A on the Accounting exam. Then, my two roommates who were the most problematic came to us and said, "Hey, we think we should change our housing situation while we can still be friends," So the two "worst offenders" prepared to move out. It was hard not to see Kevin at work, as two things really eating at me just lifted in the course of a few days.

When I started here, I thought I wanted to go into Business with an emphasis in Marketing. Since then, I've begun to spark to Accounting. I think now that that's what I will major in. It feels right now, where before, I was just floundering.

Zach

Kevin formed a tight bond with a core group of guys during his senior year at San Ramon Valley High. This group included Zach Iler, along with Grant Pisenti and Spencer Corbett. After some of the social frustrations Kevin went through during his freshman-junior years, especially when he seemed to be socially marginalized from the "cool" football crew, this group of guys felt like bedrock. Kevin finally found the guys with whom he could just be himself; a group of guys who cared about each other.

Zach went on in college to the University of Nevada Reno, along with his twin sister Chloe. We pick up Zach halfway through the second semester of his sophomore year.

You know, I never saw Kevin get down. He always stayed positive. Once in a while I would ask him how it was going, and for the most part he was always very hopeful. I remember even shortly before he lost his hair—for the third time—he said it "was going very well."

So last semester I failed a class. I didn't put in the time necessary, so I needed to retake that class this semester. I was coming up on a test and I was stressed out about it. So as I sat down to study for it I actually prayed to Kevin. I actually asked for his faith and strength. Then I got down to studying.

About an hour into my studying, I came to a problem that I remembered from the last semester, because it had stumped me then. All of a sudden, I got the chills, and I just knew how to do the problem. It clicked! I got such momentum from that that I did 3-4 more problems successfully right after it.

I aced the test the next day; got a 93.

Gustavo

Grief—or at least the way we each move through grief—is likely as individual as fingerprints.

Kevin was Gustavo's big brother, but only fifteen months separated them. Growing up, Gustavo idolized his big brother. In photo after photo of the two of them, where Kevin's eyes and smile are directed at the camera, his little brother's eyes focus adoringly on Kevin.

Somewhere along the way, I suppose sibling competition creeps into most families. I am the oldest of three. I tried to remember: was I an asshole big brother? We all name-called each other: "stupid" and "idiot" were favorites; "retard" maybe a close third, especially in our teenage years; a number of other names sprinkled in for variety in a creative, multi-faceted attack.

As they grew into their teenage years, generally, our boys remained close, doing many things together, laughing, sharing friends, playing some of the same sports, competing with each other on video games, trash-talking, as all boys that age must. But in those moments with brotherly friction, my read of Kevin's treatment of his brother was that it was more severe than the standard big-brother hierarchical ranking ritual. Kevin's inflection crossed the line between tease and venom. When Kevin called Gus "stupid" or "idiot" or a "retard" (some things change little over the generations, I suppose) or "dumbass" it sounded lacerating to me. And I would light him up for it, too.

"Kevin!" I shouted, on more than one occasion. "*Knock* it off! You have no cause to talk to your brother that way!"

"Whaaa…?!" Kevin evaded. "*He* started it !!"

"I don't care HOW it started," I doubled down. "Whatever started it doesn't justify HOW you spoke to your BROTHER!!!"

In these moments, Kevin—without fail—muttered some simpering justification for how he had spoken. I would return what I intended as the last word. Then he would mutter something else. He HAD to have the last word, however repetitive or feeble or self-righteous it came across.

Oddly—at least to me—thirty minutes after one of these biting exchanges, Kevin would appear at Gustavo's bedroom door and ask "Gus, you wanna go to In N' Out?" and off they would go. What would have left me in a simmering, festering funk, Kevin forgot soon after. And whatever injustice Gus felt at the time of the argument, he was somehow able to put behind him.

I asked him about this recently.

"Hey, Gus. I remember a lot of times Kevin would name-call in what I thought were harsh tones," I began. "How do you remember them?"

Gus had been looking me in the eye, but at that moment looked off at the wall, gathering his thoughts.

"You know, in my Psychology class, we learned about something called 'displacement.'" Gus paused. "I realized that it exactly described what Kevin was doing with me. Whatever grievance he was frustrated about—maybe football, for instance, or, to state the obvious, his battle with cancer—I was a place he could vent, even if he didn't know why he was doing it. I gave it back to him sometimes. And a few times, I even exploded at him, when I was just fed up. But I never hit him back equal to what he gave out."

I sat in stunned amazement and admiration at Gus. He had let his brother's attacks roll off of him—not all, but many—because he knew it wasn't about him (Gus). He somehow compartmentalized his own ego, and then found a place on some shelf somewhere for Kevin's attacks, and there they sat, without resentment on Gus's part, but as a series of small favors he could do for the brother he loved. And Gus figured all of this out in his *teenage* years.

I find myself humbled by both my sons, for different reasons.

Gustavo's Journal—March 17, 2019—Boston University

To Kevin:

I feel like talking to you and I have the urge to write. So that's what I'm doing. I'm thinking about what I wish I could've said to you while you were here....What we could've done together. We talked about opening that family business, and our kids growing up together....About living in the same neighborhood and having barbeques together. None of that will happen now and it feels like I'm picking up the pieces of those dreams you and I once shared. I don't know how I can let you know how much I love you and cherish all we went through together and how much it pains me that you're not here with me right now. On a personal note, I feel this absent-mindedness with people, and emotions coming from myself and I'm figuring out how to kick it out. I feel like, in a way, I never really knew you fully. I had my head so far into work, stress, and insecurity and I missed moments that matter. When you came into my room to distract me from studying, I wish I let you. When I went through your Spotify playlist and found all your music that meant so much to you I was surprised and then I felt ashamed that only then I realized how much deeper a person you were than I knew. I'm coming to realize that I feel so much shame in the way that I've lived my life, missing big moments, being too serious, not taking chances, being too logical and not expressing what I want. I am so sorry that this got in the way of me spending more time with you. I always thought you were brash, unaware, and frankly selfish, but I think there was a certain kind of love emanating from you to me that I hadn't learned to accept yet. I'm overcome with anger at myself when I think of the times that I could have gone to San Francisco to see you instead of studying, seeing my friends, seeing Isabella [Gustavo's then-girlfriend], or anything else. I know you said you wanted me to keep going but I can't forgive myself.

I'll never forget about you, Kevin, I hope you know that. Please talk to me. I don't know if I can see signs or anything but I'm trying. I hope someday that we'll see each other again. For now I try to understand the big mystery of life...or might it be more wise to live it, instead....I know it's not guaranteed.

Please forgive me for all my hard-headedness and stupidity. I don't deserve it but it kills me to think of you, and all I fucked up.

I love you, Kevin, now and forever.
Your little brother, Gustavo

Back to Work

I had left my job as the chief financial officer of a packaged foods company in May of 2018 to be with Kevin and my family. The first few months after Kevin's death, I was in no shape to commit to a new job with the kind of energy and focus I felt it deserved. In the fall of 2018, I was still in a serious funk, but I began in my mind to renew my openness to working. In November, I fielded a few inquiries from executive search firms seeking CFO candidates. By the time we installed Gustavo at Boston University in January of 2019, I returned from that trip ready to get serious about going back to work.

Over the following months, a number of CFO opportunities bubbled up. These included: Martinelli's (the sparkling cider folks); two different cannabis companies; a premium, fair-trade- sourced chocolate bar company; a vitamin company with a social responsibility mission; a company reclaiming what would otherwise be waste produce; another produce wholesaler sourcing exclusively locally; and a start-up company in sport aviation, marketing lightweight easy-to-fly airplanes. Not all of these were "right" for me, but each was intriguing enough to have a conversation or two, and some went as far as interviews with the company CEO's or members of the board of directors.

We saw Kevin at work. He always loved Martinelli's. When the first cannabis company pinged me, Marilene and I joked with each other that Kevin was creating the opportunity. That one went as far as an interview with the CEO before they offered to another candidate. When the *second* cannabis company reached out to me less than a month after the first, and it was closer to home than the first, we felt Kevin even stronger. That one, too, went to another candidate. I was not dismayed. You need to cast a wide net to be sure you catch the right fish. And, as Marilene reminded me often, "The right thing will come for us."

When we realized that the vitamin company was the same brand we had bought once for Kevin—he had a bottle of it in his dorm room at St. Mary's College—it began to seem that he was almost beating us over the head trying to get a message across.

One day at home, I was restless to the point of distraction, anxiously awaiting word from an interview I had had late the week before. I don't often get that way, and in fact in the nine months since Kevin's death I didn't once feel that kind of agitation. I actually paced the room.

Marilene sensed my tension and agitation. In the middle of deleting some things on her phone, an article popped onto her screen with the title: "There's a right time for everything." A little while later, she was flipping through a book and it fell open to a page which said: "Patience." She shared these two anecdotes with me. We both smiled in recognition, and I eased up a bit after that.

License Plates

My job search landed me at a company which produces organic meats from animals raised to sustainable and humane standards. I started there as CFO in June of 2019. In September my job took me to the company's farm and butchery near Mount Shasta in Northern California. It's a five-hour drive. I took Kevin's Toyota Tacoma truck up there. We will never sell it. Some time back, the antenna got ripped off of the truck. The radio doesn't work. So I had a long drive up, on long stretches of straight open highway, little trafficked, with time for my thoughts to wander. I could have tuned into my Spotify account to listen to music, but I opted for thoughts wandering.

As the miles unwound, and the tarmac thrummed under me, about eighty miles in I began speaking to Kevin. I do this sometimes. "How you doin' today, son? Does 'today' even mean anything, where you are? Are you still helping kids transition over, who've passed in tragic circumstances? Are you happy? Am I doing okay?"

I spoke to Kevin for several miles, passing near Davis, California on Highway 80 eastbound. I noticed a car pass by me on the left with a license plate with "K57" as part of the numbers on the plate. *Hmm*, I thought to myself. *Kevin's initial and the number on his varsity football jersey. Also part of his St. Mary's e-mail address. Noted, but not noteworthy.*

That is, not noteworthy until *another* car with a license plate with the combo of "K57" passed by *on my right side less than a minute later*!

Okay, you say. That's mildly interesting. But it's well within the scope of normal daily life. Nothing special.

Let's put a pin in that little anecdote.

I spent three days up at Shasta. On Thursday, I drove back to the Bay Area. While still on the road, I was scheduled to have a phone call at 2:00 with a candidate I wanted to hire. This candidate posed a bit of a challenge. During the interview gauntlet with various people over the preceding weeks, we had turned up some concerns. Different people were receiving different messages from the same candidate. Now, this could be communications foibles. Or it could be something deeper, a matter of integrity. If we had any integrity issues with the candidate, then it was a non-starter, and we would have to toggle to yet another candidate. If it was mere miscommunication, that was not trivial, but the candidate's other strengths might outweigh the communications flaw. So I wanted to clear some things up before extending the offer, and leading up to the planned 2:00 call I was on the fence about him, really waffling. So on the drive south from Shasta I asked Kevin for guidance. Only by now I knew to ask for *specific* guidance. I asked, "Kev, should I hire this guy? Give me a sign. Only, please give it to me so I *know* what the message is, so I don't have to guess if it's 'Yes' or if it's 'No.'"

My request made, I drove on. The miles played out, as did the time. Noon passed. I handled some work calls from my cell phone, hands free, with the earbuds in my ears so I could drive safely. I had some good calls; made progress on a few workstreams. I felt good. 1:00 rolled around. I was looking at most license plates, many road signs, occasionally the clouds, looking for something, anything that Kevin might offer me as a sign.

1:30 passed, then 1:45. At 1:55, I was nearing the time of my call, and I had seen nothing definitive. I was beginning to resign myself to the fact that I was not going to hear from Kevin on my candidate.

At three minutes before 2:00, a car passed by on my left. I glanced at the license plate, then did a double-take and looked again to be sure what I'd seen.

The license plate on that car read "570YES."

In case that didn't register, that was Kevin's varsity football number, #57, followed by "O YES."

Once I confirmed—after my double-take—what I had seen, I slapped my steering wheel with a loud smack and shouted a triumphant "Hah!" "Thank you, son!" I offered. But a moment later, I was overcome. It struck me so hard that he was right there with me, but I couldn't see or touch him. He heard everything I said and answered so earnestly, so *urgently.* How *present* he was, and oddly it deepened my pangs of missing him. I knew then that he was close, but I couldn't touch him. I cried for a minute. It was far easier to imagine him far off in heaven in spirit than right here with me, and me unable to see, hear, or touch him.

I did hire that candidate and he turned out to be a very strong hire. There were communications foibles, but his strengths far outweighed any issues.

The day after I saw the license plate, something dawned on me. California license plates have seven characters: one number; followed by three letters; followed by three numbers. It had been that way for years. How many years? I looked it up. The state stopped issuing six-digit plates in 1980.

Furthermore, after they converted to seven-character plates, in the mid-eighties California converted from blue-background plates to ones with white reflective backgrounds. The "570YES" plate was definitely a white-background plate. I can't say the make, model, or year of the car that had the plate; I was so blown away by the message itself that the car didn't make an impression. It was a light color, I know that. And I'm sure that it wasn't more than twenty years old. I notice cars. I would have noted it if the car was an older model. So the point is, six-character plates stopped by 1980, and six-character plates were on blue backgrounds, not white ones. Yet my message was six characters on the white reflective background.

So it must have been a personalized—or vanity—license plate. Could the owner of that car have chosen "570YES" as their personalized plate, because "570YES" had some special meaning to that owner, that the rest of us can't fathom? That's the most probable reason for the plate that I saw.

A little more research turned up that there's about fourteen million cars registered in California. So let's play skeptic. Which is more plausible: that that one—and there's only one—out of maybe fourteen million license plates in California should randomly show up at my left three minutes before the "deadline" of my request to Kevin? or, simply, Kevin answered my request, in so specific a way as to leave no doubt of the interpretation of the message, *exactly* as I had asked of him, and right up to almost the last minute of the time where that answer would be useful to me, in a manner so fitting his personality? Then, if we place this anecdote in the context of what happened on the outbound leg of this trip, recalling the two "K57" license plates that had "embraced" me on the way north, it seems to me that the case for randomness or coincidence gets harder and harder to make. Yes, that's *exactly* what it was: the ultimate "personalized" license plate. It was a personalized answer to a personal question, between father and son.

But let's try to exhaust any remaining skeptic's scenarios. Could I maybe simply have missed—or forgotten—a leading digit on a non-personalized plate? Also theoretically possible, of course. Even if I did, I don't think it invalidates the impact of the six characters that I just described. But let's pursue this anyhow. Remember: the license plate convention on non-commercial vehicles in California for decades now is seven characters: one digit followed by three letters, followed by three more digits. First of all, this was a passenger car, not a commercial vehicle. I saw—and I am absolutely certain of this—three numbers followed by three letters. So if you believe me when I describe what I saw, and you wish to assume that I just overlooked a leading digit, then the order is flipped. Say I forgot the leading digit. Then what I ought to have seen would be three letters followed by three numbers (assuming it was not a personalized plate, as described above). But it was three numbers first, not three letters first, so the sequencing is flipped from that on a normal passenger car, even one with a seven-digit plate. So this hypothesis, that I simply forgot a leading digit on a seven-digit plate, plays out as unlikely.

Could I simply have seen what I wanted to see, "manufactured" this vision, in my mind? Actually, this possibility is far more plausible than the random one teed up two paragraphs before this. Hey, I'm a grief-stricken father, desperate to have a sign from the son I miss so much. Stranger things have happened, you might say.

It's difficult to prove my—or anyone's—lucidity or sanity. I could tell you I'm a chief financial officer, a husband of twenty-three years, a father, a homeowner, sending my other son to Boston University, never been arrested, never been in therapy, not a substance-abuser. But you could say, "Yeah, but there's plenty of crazy CFO's out there." And you'd be right. I've *met* some of them.

But these are all reference-points into the world of our *heads*. I think we are applying the wrong tool to the job. For this, we need to seek the answers to our questions elsewhere.

At the end of the day, how does what happened here resonate with you in your *heart*? I think far more of our answers are there, but we have been conditioned to revere the mind. We respect the intellect over intuition. We prioritize science over art. We give more credence to the material than the emotional. We are out of balance, and our physical world is worse off for that. We need to restore balance between heart and mind, for the well-being of people and planet.

Four days later I told this story to a small group of people. One of them pointed out to me that it was 1:57—three minutes before 2:00—when that car passed me. Jeez, how did I miss that on the first go, and for so many days afterwards? So rather than trying to hang me in suspense until the last minute, perhaps Kevin was simply repeating the 57 theme.

In fact, as this possibility crystallized for me, I began to think "How could it be *other* than that?" The two "K57" license plates, one minute apart, on my drive up to Shasta. Then the one-in-fourteen million "570 YES" license plate, right at the deadline of my need for an answer to my request, at 1:57 p.m.! It's almost too elegant to dismiss. And it's pure Kevin: "How ya like me NOW?!"

License plates seem to be a convenient conduit through which Kevin communicates. Two weeks after the stunning message on my way back from Shasta, I noted that the car in front of me in downtown Walnut Creek near the Trader Joe's had a plate which read "7KEV570." I had not made any special request. And I debated: Random coincidence? or tickle? It felt like a tickle. That 570 appearing again, so soon after the Shasta miracle, and coupled with "KEV," simply felt like Kevin winking at me, reminding me he was around; showing off, even. But it also felt like a piece of validation after the fact. By that I mean it felt like a small, simple reinforcement that the Shasta experience was no coincidence, and that my son had me in mind even when I wasn't directly asking him for something. I smiled and thanked him.

A couple months later, Marilene and I were returning home from some errand or another through downtown Walnut Creek. At a stoplight, she gasped and said "Oh, my God!! Kevin!" I whipped my head this way and that, trying to figure out what she was talking about. She pointed at a car one lane over to our left and about eighty feet in front of us. The car was a Nissan 370Z. Its license plate said "EYE AMM."

I looked over at Marilene, the unasked question on my face.

"Just a half-hour ago," she began, breathlessly, "I asked Kevin to help Gus." Gustavo was going through a tough patch at school back in Boston. We believe he still has a way to go in processing his own grief at Kevin's passing. She continued, "And now, here, half an hour later, I see this license plate! It's Kevin. There can be no doubt!"

Unlike my Shasta or "7KEV570" anecdotes, this one had a witness: me. We both saw that license plate. This anecdote resonates with multiple others—some told in this book, but many others just treasured in our memories—where Kevin gave definitive responses to requests we've each made of him. These messages respond to the requests we've made, to be sure. But it is so much more than that. He delivers such heartfelt messages, in ways so personal and loving and comforting, triggering such amazement and such...*recognition*...that we haven't the slightest shred of doubt that it is him. He forges messages so forcefully and so *him* that the word "maybe" never crosses our minds, and that's clearly his intent.

I thought this chapter was complete. But on the evening of Friday, February 21, 2020 Marilene and I were on the way to meet some friends for dinner at a restaurant some seven miles from home. Our day had left us fraught. Gustavo continues to struggle with buried emotions connected with Kevin and us. He is on a journey with which we—or anyone else—can only help so much. We can support, advise, suggest. But he must open the doors and take the actions, and the emotions will not subside or go away. They will insist on coming out, and not always in ways that others will understand. Marilene and I were a bit tense and wrung out as we drove to meet our friends.

We were on our way to meet our friends the Tengs at a Moroccan restaurant. We had never been there. So we entered the address in Marilene's phone (the phone she had inherited and adapted from Kevin) and allowed Google Maps to direct us as I drove. Google Maps did not direct me to the freeway, which I assumed would be the most direct and speediest route to the restaurant. But I didn't pay that too much mind, as it was close to rush hour, and perhaps Google Maps was taking that into account, and simply steering me to another route to avoid traffic.

As the Google Maps guidance played out, we drove down darker and more remote avenues and streets. At one point, the electronic voice steered us on a narrow, two-lane winding road through forest. *This doesn't feel right,* we murmured. We expected to end up in a commercial zone nested within a suburban surrounding, where a handful of restaurants, dry cleaners, and other retail services served the local community. A brooding, narrow, winding forest road was not on the agenda when the evening started. But we went with it, hesitantly trusting the voice.

After a few minutes, the narrow forest road connected with a throughway with two lanes in each direction. This appeared like an artery which might after all connect us with what we expected. Three or four minutes more, and the Google Maps voice indicated that we were a couple turns from our destination.

Just then, I looked up ahead of me. The car directly in front of us was a metallic silver Lexus. Its license plate: "7KEV570"!

I exclaimed to Marilene, "Look! Remember that plate I told you about a couple weeks after Shasta?! It's the *same car!*" Marilene saw it, too. She was moved to tears, briefly. So *this* plate now has two witnesses.

To be sure, that Lexus belongs to a resident who lives within the metro area we inhabit. This spotting was about seven or so miles from my earlier one. It's certainly within the scope of chance that we might encounter that—or any given local plate—more than once. But as we briefly reflected on our angst about Gustavo, our repeated entreaties to Kevin to help his brother, our frazzled day, and finally the distinctly odd route-guidance we were given, by Kevin's former phone, to get to the restaurant, it was just too much. Kevin is at work, and he offered us a message of comfort. And comfort it was.

But this book is not titled *Relentless* for nothing.

Just nine days further on, on Sunday, March 1, 2020, Marilene and I had breakfast in Walnut Creek. I was in a restless, frazzled mood. Our politics was in a severe mess and had me tense. This was also in a time when the coronavirus was just shaping up as a real global health threat and we seemed ill-prepared to deal with it. My work situation was changeable. Gustavo was struggling, and we had been hearing of several other young men and women his age who were facing anxiety, depression, or other emotional challenges. Everything felt...whacked. So this particular morning I felt agitated and adrift, and unsure what to do about it.

After breakfast, Marilene and I agreed to go to the gym across town. Maybe a good workout would take the edge off, burn off some of the agitation I felt. This would turn out to be one of the last weekends for a while that the gym was even open, due to the concerns about the virus.

Upon arriving at the gym and checking in, Marilene and I each peeled off to our respective locker rooms. Marilene has a favorite locker. But it was taken, this particular Sunday. The ladies' locker room was fairly full. Marilene's second and third locker preferences were occupied, as well. So she selected another one. She placed her clothes and gear in this locker, before deciding against it for reasons unknown, yanking her stuff out, and finally choosing *yet another* locker. Happily, this locker was vacant.

Vacant, that is, except for a small scrap of brown paper. Marilene picked it up. The scrap had a staple in it: a dry-cleaning tag, the kind that they loop through a buttonhole and staple the ends together to identify one's shirt or blouse. Marilene peered at the little scrap. On one side, it had the numbers "10" and "57." On the flip side, "570."

Helping Parents Heal

"Look around this room," Bryan said. "You have something special going on here."

I swept my gaze around the room. Maybe sixteen people milled around in pairs or in small groups, chatting animatedly, earnestly. Some exchanged numbers. Others leaned in to hear someone share a story. Still others—eyes widened and lit as if about to laugh—smiled, held their breath, and awaited the payoff line. Bryan was right; there was a palpable buzz in the room. People did not want to leave, even though we had wrapped up maybe twenty minutes before.

This was Sunday, January 27, 2020 at the Danville Grange meeting/ community hall. The San Francisco Bay Area chapter of Helping Parents Heal met there. The group meets on the last Sunday of each month from 10 a.m. to noon. The Grange building goes back at least eighty years, with creaky hardwood floors and rustic casement windows, the kind you have to heave to slide up, and you need to mind the splinters when you do.

Today's meeting attracted twenty-two people. Just six months before, we had eight. Various couples and individuals came up to us afterward, saying how grateful they were that we had started the group, and that they'd see us next month.

When we look back and retrace the threads that connected us to Helping Parents Heal, we can't escape the feeling that we were somehow steered there:

- ✻ At a spiritual healer in Brazil in December 2017, Marilene learned about crystal beds. Kevin used one there. (A crystal bed beams colored light through quartz crystals, aimed at stimulating your seven chakras.)
- ✻ After returning from Brazil, Marilene researched crystal beds in California.
- ✻ This search connected Marilene with a woman in nearby Lafayette (just a few miles from our current house). This woman—Kathryn de Silva—had one of the few crystal beds in the Bay Area, which she keeps at home.
- ✻ Marilene reached out to Kathryn and arranged a visit to her crystal bed for Kevin. Kathryn was most kind and accommodating.
- ✻ As Kevin relaxed in the crystal bed with the alternating colored lights dancing over him, Marilene chatted with Kathryn in a nearby room. Marilene later described this chat as "Two hours in twenty minutes," it was so jammed with information. As Kathryn heard more about Kevin's situation, she suggested some additional resources that Marilene might seek out.

Marilene and Kevin visited Kathryn once or twice more before he passed. Kathryn stayed in touch after that, too, and we became friends. She began to suggest other resources. One of these was a medium named

Suzanne Giesemann. And in researching Suzanne Giesemann, Marilene stumbled onto Helping Parents Heal.

HPH is a national, non-profit organization. Its mission is to support grieving parents. It was started by Elizabeth Boisson and Mark Ireland in 2012. Both Elizabeth and Mark have lost children. In fact, Elizabeth lost two: a daughter in 1991 and a son in 2009. What distinguishes HPH from other grief support organizations is that it promotes open discussion of the afterlife, and how our passed loved ones still stay with us and interact with us if we know how to look for them.

As Marilene studied more about HPH, she found that the only California chapter of the national organization was in San Diego. An idea took root with her: What if I start a Northern California chapter?

Over a few weeks, Marilene contacted the national HPH organization for information and guidance. In parallel, she test-drove with me the idea of starting the SF Bay Area chapter. I told her that it was a terrific idea, and that I would help her in any way I could. She also reached out to another local mother - Beverly Wilson - who we knew personally who had also lost her son Mason within six months of Kevin, to see if she wished to co-found the group.

As it turned out, Beverly knew someone connected with the Danville Grange, and she was able to obtain a room for us there for free, two hours the morning of the last Sunday of each month. She placed announcements about the new chapter out on Facebook. And away we went.

The first meeting of the SF Bay Area chapter of HPH happened in August 2019. We drew six other parents. With Marilene and me, we had eight. We went around the room, sharing a little about our sons and daughters, what caused them to pass, and how we were dealing with grief. In addition, in *this* group, everyone had stories of signs they had received from their passed children.

Over a couple months, two or three couples migrated over to this HPH group from the former grief group we had attended in Walnut Creek from November 2018 to June 2019. These people—like us—felt that their children were still with them, still communicating with them. And they—like us—wanted to be around others sharing similar experiences.

Some of the testimonials were quite startling. One woman who had lost her daughter shared that a blue jay—her daughter's favorite bird—flew in and perched on her shoulder one day in the back yard as she was speaking with a friend about...her daughter. One couple shared that they were arguing while standing in their (passed) daughter's room. From a shelf nearby, a little toy rattled: a plastic plate with plastic cupcakes on it; their daughter's favorite toy. They dismissed it and resumed the argument. Then the toy rattled *again.* The couple decided that they had better settle the argument.

One couple's son sends hawks. They had lost him to cancer at twenty-three. A couple months after he passed, the family took a trip. Standing in front of a post-fence overlooking a bluff near the coast in Santa Barbara, someone said, "Hey, let's take a family picture." They lined up with their backs to the water as one person prepared to snap the photo. Then the photographer said, "I think someone wants to get in on the act." The gang looked to their right. A hawk had landed on the fence just a few feet from the family, facing toward the camera! A few months after that, as the mother went to greet a friend at the front door of their home, she spied a hawk perched just a few feet away on the hood of her car in the driveway, right by the hood ornament. "What hawk *ever does* things like that?" she asks the group.

Those are just a few of at least dozens of anecdotes shared by the parents in the group. Not all of the stories are knock-your-socks-off compelling. But about three-quarters of them are! Frequently, our departed children play tricks or jokes on us. For a group of grieving parents, we actually laugh quite a bit. One of the reasons most of the stories are so persuasive is that the *personalities* seem to come through so vividly. Kevin comes across forcefully, persistently, as he was in life. One couple's grandson regularly hides things or flickers the lights or opens and closes the garage door, consistent with his mischievous ways. Another couple who lost their son to suicide receive regular messages and signs of comfort, as if to assuage the guilt and despair that parents in that situation almost always feel.

We cry, too. One young couple lost their daughter at three years old. How to extract meaning from that—or from any—of our stories? I told this couple that a medium once told me that Kevin was fulfilling a "soul contract." He *signed up* to go before us. Why? I can't say for certain, but if it was to open our minds or maybe open some doors for us, *that* is definitely happening. Maybe it was solely for us to open more to the spiritual side of life. Maybe it was only about forming this group, which gives immense comfort to people really hurting. Even as a hypothetical narrative, that is extremely comforting. When I couple that narrative with things that have happened to us, with the people we've met, and weave it all together, I do get this feeling of flow, as if in a smooth current bearing me and Marilene on to some wonderful place. If indeed Kevin fulfilled his soul contract, and it was for me, Marilene and Gustavo to grow, then what a loving sacrifice he made for us. That would lend meaning to an otherwise senseless—in our wrought minds—event.

Bryan saw it. We had fed each other. We had together spun up the energy of everyone in the room. As I sustained my gaze and my smile at the group, several hugged each other goodbye; even some who had only just met for the first time. Many who had arrived downcast clearly now vibrated at the other end of the spectrum. Gradually, they filed out, thanking us and saying, "See you next month, for sure!

I turned back to Bryan, gave his shoulder a slight squeeze, and said, "You're right. We do have something special here. It's a great group. And thank you for being a part of it. I hope we see you next month!"

Tribute and Transformation

This began in desperation. I was desperate to do something with my grief. I started trying to describe it. I wrote from a deep hole, purging, trying to transmit what it feels like when the world implodes and folds in on itself. Overnight, I was unhooked from everything I had ever learned, trusted, or counted on. The ground retreated from my feet. Nothing made sense. Nothing mattered. My insides emptied, and for months I wrote with a gaping, vacant void right through me. The rest of me? Dull flesh.

Even during those darkest months, we received glimpses of Kevin, and he did many things to try to lift us. And it helped. We began to believe that perhaps it doesn't end with death after all, and that he continued, that we *all* continue, and that we would see him again. He showed up in so many different ways: through animals, birds, and insects; "speaking" to friends; through electronic devices; in visitation dreams; and by answering our—and other people's—requests. We might have dismissed three or four such occurrences. But soon we had too many to dismiss, and so many delivered so forcefully, that we could not rationalize them away. Nor would we rationalize them away, as to do so would be to turn our back on our son and his loving, magnificent efforts.

Believing became *knowing* with the epic day in San Francisco at the show with psychic medium Bill Philipps, four months after Kevin passed. For me and Marilene, that is the day against which *Before* and *After* will always be marked, the rest of our lives.

With Kevin's "interventions"—some so insistent it's almost as if he's knocking on my forehead "Hell-OOOooo?!"—it's clear that he wants me to *know and feel*, not just *believe*. I am reminded of Maya Angelou. She said, "*I have learned that people will forget what you said. They will forget what you did. But they will never forget how you made them feel.*" The gift that Kevin has given me, through the journey described in this book, is that now I *know and feel* there's more, and I have no doubt anymore. And if I would be convinced with the dial at 10, he steps it up to 30, to be sure I get the message. Once again, that is pure Kevin; he is not a master of—or perhaps has little use for—subtlety.

Let the comfort of that soak into you for a minute. If death is nothing to fear, how differently would you live your life? If you *know* that your passed loved ones are with you, happy and freed and supporting you, then what's to fear or dread? Doubt and fear can find no harbor with you. How liberating is *that*?! How fulfilled can you be if all that baggage is lifted, if you begin to get out of your own way?

If the reader has lost someone dear, some advice I would offer follows. Now, as we've said in these pages, grief is very personal, very individual. There is no one right or wrong way to handle it. But I *know* your departed loved one does not want you to dwell in despair. So for what they're worth, some things that I know have helped me and others:

* ***Cry. Feel.*** It'll come out sooner or later. It's actually healthy to have good, deep, sobbing cries.
* ***Get out into nature.*** Hike, walk a trail, sail a boat. Drive to Inspiration Point.
* ***Do something physical,*** something creative. Garden. Chop wood. Paint. Sculpt.
* ***Write.*** A journal. A diary. A dream diary. A novel. An essay on grief. These first four points are all about release. Let the feeling out. Express it.
* ***Read.*** After what you've been through, you may never be more open, more of a sponge, for new material and new ideas. Embrace it.
* ***Get support:*** a grief group; a grief counselor. Helping Parents Heal. Something on a schedule. Something with people who know and understand what you're going through. It will surprise you how helpful this is.
* ***Talk.*** Keep your loved one alive and ask others to do so, as well. And talk to your departed loved one. Ask him or her for things.
* ***Be open and aware.*** If/when you suspect you just received a sign, trust it.
* ***Lean on friends.*** And be with them. This one may feel challenging, as someone grief-stricken just may not feel up to socializing. But you may find that your good friends *want* to be supportive, if you'll just let them in. Think about how you feel when someone trusts you; it's a good feeling, isn't it? Why would you withhold that trust from someone who would feel good if they can help?
* ***Question.*** It's all up for grabs. Nothing you thought or assumed turns out to be true. Question, inquire. Re-think. And as the universe offers you new ideas, test them. And feel whether they resonate for you/with you.

I have come to a place where I believe that grief can be...a giant unlock. To say "*No pain; no gain*" is too trite. But it may carry the grain of truth that all clichés do.

But beyond that, Kevin does not want me to grieve. It pains him when we're pained. Our thoughts and feelings ripple out there. When we've received signs from him, he always comes from a place of joy, and he always offers us reassurance and support, and always lovingly. (Well, he *was* upset the one time when Marilene lost his/her phone. But he helped us find it the next day, and even his irritation was pure...him!) I feel him as an optimistic, supporting presence, even a joking one sometimes, another indication that his personality persists.

So Kevin's transformation has happened, or is underway. And he is helping me with my own transformation, pulling me even now. Perhaps he is pulling these words out *through* me...I am still trying to learn what is me and what is something deeper, or what is something *outside* me. I thought I knew once, but this opening to something broader, deeper, and behind the curtain, raises that question almost every day.

I've never felt more anticipation for a journey.

As I did at his eulogy, I raise my glass to our warrior son Kevin. Only at his eulogy, it was goodbye. Now it's "Thank you for your courage, Thanks for continuing to show me the way. Thanks for being with us."

You amaze me, son, and I will love you through time.

THE END...FOR NOW!

CPSIA information can be obtained
at www.ICGtesting.com
Printed in the USA
BVHW020443131020
590835BV00025B/521